POWER OF SAIL

Paul Grellong

BROADWAY PLAY PUBLISHING INC
New York
www.broadwayplaypublishing.com
info@broadwayplaypublishing.com

Cover art by Justin Bettman

First edition: February 2025
I S B N: 979-8-88856-047-1

Book design: Marie Donovan
Page make-up: Adobe InDesign
Typeface: Palatino

The World Premiere of POWER OF SAIL opened
on 15 March 2019 at The Warehouse Theatre (Mike
Sablone, Producing Artistic Director; Jason D Johnson,
Managing Director) in Greenville, SC. The cast and
creative contributors were:

CHARLES NICHOLS ....Rob Kahn
AMY KATZ..Kerrie Seymour
BAXTER FORREST...Sean Michael
LUCAS POOLE................................Christopher Paul Smith
MAGGIE ROSEN...................................... Anna Abhau Elliott
HARRIS/FRANK .... Andy Croston

Director...Jackson Gay
Stage Manager ....Louise M Ochart
Scenic Designer .... Shannon Robert
Costume Designer.. Kendra Johnson
Lighting Designer...Tony Penna
Sound Designer .... Marc Gwinn
Props Designer..Cassidy Bowles
Assistant Director...................................Mallory Pellegrino
Assistant Stage Manager......................................Grace Arndt

POWER OF SAIL had its West Coast premiere at
The Geffen Playhouse (Matt Shakman, Artistic
Director; Gil Gates, Jr, Executive Director) running
from 8 February-27 March 2022. The cast and creative
contributors were:

CHARLES NICHOLS ....Bryan Cranston
AMY KATZ... Amy Brenneman
BAXTER FORREST...Brandon Scott
LUCAS POOLE..Seth Numrich
MAGGIE ROSEN...Tedra Millan
QUINN HARRIS *(thru March 20)* .. Donna Simone Johnson
    (after March 20)............. Safiya Fredericks
FRANK SULLIVAN....................................Hugo Armstrong

understudies...............Hugo Armstrong, Safiya Fredericks
    Zach Kenney, Sharon Sharth,
    Sarah Traisman, Hari Williams

Director..Weyni Mengesha
Producer... Daryl Roth
Scenic Designer ....Rachel Myers
Costume Designer....................................Samantha C Jones
Lighting Designer... Lap Chi Chu
Original music, Sound Designer................. Jonathan Snipes
Dramaturg ....Mike Sablone
Production Stage Manager......................... J Jason Daunter
Ass't Stage Manager (thru 11 March) .....Lizzie Thompson
    (after 11 March)...................Kesia Ross
Casting Director ....Phyllis Schuringa, CSA

POWER OF SAIL had its UK premiere at Menier
Chocolate Factory Theatre (David Babani, Artistic
Director; Tom Siracusa, General Manager) in London
running from 20 March-12 May 2024. The cast and
creative contributors were:

CHARLES NICHOLS ....Julian Ovenden
AMY KATZ..Tanya Franks
BAXTER FORREST (*thru May 5*) .... Giles Terera
                        (*after May 5*)..........................Syrus Lowe
LUCAS POOLE..Michael Benz
MAGGIE ROSEN...Katie Bernstein
QUINN HARRIS... Georgia Landers
FRANK SULLIVAN..Paul Rider

Director... Dominic Dromgoole
Co-producer .... Daryl Roth
Set & Costume Designer .... Paul Farnsworth
Lighting Designer...Oliver Fenwick
Sound Designer .... Ella Wahlström
Video Designer.. Leo Flint
Dramaturg ....Mike Sablone
Company Stage Manager ....Jonathan Gosling
Deputy Stage Manager...................................Roan Torrance
Assistant Stage Manager.................................. Bella Kelaidi

AUTHOR'S NOTE

In the summer of 2017 I began revising an old draft of
this play. My friend Mike Sablone, Producing Artistic
Director of The Warehouse Theatre, encouraged me
to look again at a script I hadn't touched in years. I'm
eternally grateful that he did. There was, to understate
things, quite a lot of work to do. A year and a half later
in March 2019, the Warehouse produced the world
premiere.

POWER OF SAIL is set in 2019. When I've been asked,
I offer two reasons why I've never adjusted the year
for subsequent productions. The first is specifically
COVID-related. I didn't write a script dealing with life
during or after the pandemic (to whatever extent we're
in the "after"). The second reason has to do with the
characters' psychologies. The way they approach what
happens in this play involves a mindset different from
those who, in the summer of 2020, would have seen
the long overdue yet still decidedly unfinished racial
reckoning in this country and around the world. These
characters would bring a different perspective to the
play's incidents and a different set of behaviors in their
wake. It remains important to me that this story is set
at the doorstep of these two seismic events.

In every iteration of the play, two things have
remained unchanged: the central premise and the
structure. First, a sentence on the premise. Esteemed
Harvard professor, a self-identifying liberal, invites a

Holocaust-denying White nationalist to give a lecture on campus and participate in a debate.

As to the structure, I set out to write a thriller about the accepted boundaries of speech and the lines between facts and falsehoods, presented in a circular structure that manipulates time to blur those lines. White nationalism and Holocaust denial distort truth and omit facts to achieve their destructive aims. I intended to turn that weapon around, repurposing their tools of distortion and omission to the script's dramatic advantage.

I also had another, more personal reason for structuring the play in this manner.

There is a tradition in Yiddish and Hebrew storytelling that tales are not wrapped up in a redemptive fashion with characters having an epiphany or being "saved." Rather, stories' endings often signal a continuation, are notably abrupt, or indeed circle back to the beginning. As a Jewish writer, it felt fitting—urgent, even—to step into the slipstream of that tradition.

My hope is that readers and audience members come along on this ride and engage as deeply as they see fit, in their own ways, with this one piece of a charged, complex puzzle. What follows, ideally, is debate. This play is not prescriptive, nor does it provide easy, tidy answers. Such answers don't exist because these are not easy, tidy questions. Or times.

I am writing this author's note in the fall of 2024. Late fall. A certain kind of circle has closed in the United States, and we find ourselves on what for many of us feels like unsettlingly remembered ground. We are back at the beginning, uttering a familiar refrain.

November 2024

CHARACTERS & SETTING

CHARLES NICHOLS, *White, 50s*
AMY KATZ, *White, Jewish, 50s*
BAXTER FORREST, *Black, 30s*
LUCAS POOLE, *White, late 20s*
MAGGIE ROSEN, *White, Jewish, late 20s*
QUINN HARRIS, *Black, 30s*
FRANK SULLIVAN, *White, 50s*

Place: Scenes take place in an office on the Harvard campus; a bar; two homes; and a train platform in New Hampshire.

Time: Fall, 2019.

Structure: The play first moves forward through the odd-numbered scenes (1, 3, 5).

The play then continues with the even-numbered scenes taking place in reverse order (6, 4, 2). The effect should be that of a round-trip journey.

Scene One

(In darkness. Hear the shouting of protestors. Youthful angry voices, impassioned, straining. Chants such as "No Nazis, no KKK, no fascist USA!" The sound grows until it is very loud.)

(Lights up on Professor CHARLES NICHOLS' office. The tall shelves are exploding with papers and books. On a table against the wall sits a coffee pot, currently switched on. There are two large windows that look out onto the campus quad.)

(In one corner is an oak stand on top of which rests an impressive model of a sailboat; hand-constructed, well-maintained. The model is encased in a glass display box.)

(CHARLES, back against the wall, sneaks looks out his window, taking care not to be seen.)

(The office door opens. AMY enters. CHARLES didn't hear the door over the chanting. AMY regards CHARLES for a moment. Her look has pity in it.)

AMY: Charlie.

CHARLES: *(Startled)* Jesus.

AMY: Sorry…

CHARLES: What took you so long?

AMY: Pushing through your groupies downstairs.

CHARLES: America's youth.

AMY: Well. So, listen—

CHARLES: They're out there, and this whole mess, because someone leaked the list of speakers. *That's* the issue. Not the list, not who's on it. So, who leaked the list?

AMY: Okay. First. I don't know. But have you seen this—

CHARLES: Hang on—you said your office would look into it.

AMY: Charles—and they *are* looking—but—

CHARLES: Great. And. What have they found?

AMY: Since it leaked last night? Nothing.

CHARLES: A dean should be able to throw her weight around, get things done quickly.

AMY: Uh-huh. Did you see the *Globe* this morning?

CHARLES: No.

(AMY *hands* CHARLES *a newspaper. It's open to a certain page.*)

CHARLES: (*Reads*) Oh please. This is—and this is online too?

AMY: Unfortunately.

CHARLES: (*Reads*) "Professor Charles Nichols is, at best, an apologist for and, at worst, a sympathizer with White nationalists, neo-Nazis, and Klansmen." (*Looks up*) This man is a celebrated civil rights attorney. Why's he coming after *me*? I'm one of the good guys. I know him, by the way. He used to hit on Diane at dinner parties, so…

AMY: We need to talk about damage control.

CHARLES: Who leaked the list? That's the damage. Control *that*.

AMY: We will find out, we will do that, we're just not gonna do that first.

(AMY's *cell phone rings. She fishes it out of her bag, looks at the screen. Disappointed, she silences it.*)

CHARLES: Do you need to—

AMY: No. Not the call I'm waiting for.

(CHARLES *eyes* AMY *with sympathy.*)

CHARLES: Let me get you a cup of coffee.

AMY: No, thanks, I've had plenty. Up since three.

CHARLES: How is Eliot today?

AMY: The same. He's not sleeping. Waiting on this blood work is hell. (*Pause*) He told me you called him.

CHARLES: I missed my favorite gimlet-drinker.

AMY: Thank you. His friends are checking in less.

CHARLES: He didn't mention that.

AMY: Would *you*?

(*The chanting outside dies down, replaced by a single orator on a bullhorn, muffled and inaudible here.*)

CHARLES: Oh thank God.

(*As* CHARLES *crosses to the window to look out,* AMY *can see that his knee is troubling him.*)

AMY: *Still* with the knee.

CHARLES: Mm. Comes and goes.

AMY: (*Pause*) You have to write a statement.

CHARLES: Oh, do I? To what, to say…I changed my mind? I no longer see the value in publicly dismantling a racist because the *students*—that, that some might get their feelings hurt? This is a university. Ideas get debated here. I have nothing to apologize for.

AMY: It's 2019. That's not gonna cut it with these kids.

CHARLES: Screw these kids. These babies. Think they can never know offense, never be challenged. They wouldn't last a day in the `60s. They show up to class in pajamas. Holding pillows. Pillows! They sing songs from Disney cartoons in the hallway.

AMY: You'd prefer the choral works of Bach?

CHARLES: I had a plan. None of this would have happened if I could have announced the series the proper way.

AMY: You invited a literal White nationalist to campus, so I'm not sure that's the case.

CHARLES: Well, I am. Just look at the rest of the names. Carver is the only voice from the far-right. A couple of genuine lefties. Everyone else, straight down the middle. So, so, let's not—please do me that favor, let's not pretend I'm hosting a rogues' gallery of Nazis.

AMY: You seriously want—*tell* me, you think it's a *good* idea for Carver's talk to be simulcast on WGBH, posted on the Harvard YouTube channel?

CHARLES: This symposium is mine. I created it. Fifteen years. I set the speakers.

AMY: Why are you making my life so much harder? When you know, you actually know what—

CHARLES: I do know.

AMY: (*Over him*) On a day-to-day, what I'm dealing with. When it's—whether it's at home, or the endless fires I have to put out here, constantly.

CHARLES: Yes, I—

AMY: Twenty years, we've known each other. We're friends. We problem-solve together. So, how is it you've—and it's baffling to me—that you've become my biggest problem?

CHARLES: I'm not the problem. *They're* making this a problem.

(Outside, the end of the orator's bullhorn speech is met by a wave of roaring cheers and applause. Someone bangs loudly on a drum. CHARLES and AMY are both drawn to the window. They peer out, then exchange a look.)

CHARLES: And they've added a rhythm section.

AMY: Mm. *(Pause)* And please, let me, just—I need to tell you that this has been frustrating to me. To talk to you about this. As a Jewish person. I wish you could step out of your own, your, your perspective, and see that this has always been a very bad and honestly offensive idea. But you're so locked in…

CHARLES: Look. Wait. Look. And I understand that, I hear you, I do. But inviting him here, Carver, is about illuminating—all right? Illuminating how societies, how communities, create an atmosphere in which ideas, ideas in bad faith, lies, can thrive.

AMY: You don't need to bring a White nationalist here to show that. And just to enter it into the record, don't even get me *started* on the raging misogyny of their movement, which, we can table that for another day, but I mean *please*. Okay? Carver practically grew up in the Klan, he denies the Holocaust. When he speaks, it's hate speech.

CHARLES: The answer to hate speech is more speech.

AMY: Your age-old mantra.

CHARLES: Well, it's true.

AMY: Not with Nazis, it's not.

CHARLES: That's bullshit. People need to face this threat. Look it in the eye. Carver is the enemy. So, why is he—him and people like him—why are they gaining such prominence?

AMY: Maybe because they keep getting invited to speak at major universities.

CHARLES: Listen. Carver is good-looking, dresses well, warm smile…he's tailor-made for cable news and the online content factories. At thirty-one years old Carver is changing their movement. Thirty-one. A kid!

AMY: You just finished saying our teenage students aren't grown up enough. Now this Klansman in his thirties is "a kid". Which is it?

CHARLES: Can you focus, please? This invitation is not about supporting the cause of White nationalism, but if you want to destroy the negatives in the darkroom, you open up the door and let some light in. Right? At a moment—in a country—awash in ideological filth, more speech is the disinfectant. *I'm* the disinfectant. Me. I can pull this idiot's pants down on a stage that matters. He speaks. Afterward, I debate him, his ideas don't hold up. He can't win.

AMY: He doesn't need them to hold up. Just being here is the win.

CHARLES: Not after I'm done. A full dismantling. To say nothing, by the way, of the fact that this is a First Amendment issue.

AMY: We're at a private university, so no, it's not. And *this* private university has decided that you are to back down and write a statement.

CHARLES: If you force me to disinvite Carver, I will cancel the symposium.

AMY: *(Pause)* The president is trying to be respectful of your position. Of the series' history.

CHARLES: And I appreciate that. But this is happening.

(Beat)

AMY: Can I say something? As someone who cares about you? Don't take my head off. *(Pause)* I think this is about Jameelah.

CHARLES: What?

AMY: Not literally "about" her, but maybe what she…
represents.

CHARLES: What the hell are you talking about?

AMY: You have a younger colleague. A female
colleague…

CHARLES: It has nothing to do with her.

AMY: A younger, female colleague whose book is
popular. Who goes on MSNBC and talks to Rachel
Maddow…

CHARLES: You think I'm jealous.

AMY: Are you jealous?

CHARLES: No. My last book did fine.

AMY: Nobody read the book, Charlie. And that's okay.

CHARLES: The book did fine.

AMY: It was a little dense.

CHARLES: You're dense! The book was good!

(AMY *picks up a copy of the book from his shelf.*)

AMY: I didn't say it wasn't good! It just…runs long.

CHARLES: When the subject matter calls for it, calls for
heft, then—

AMY: (*Reading its title*) "Bedrock Beneath the
Crossroads: Movement Structures and the Liberal
Foundation of the Warren Court, 1953-1959." (*Pause*)
"Volume *One*."

CHARLES: I hope you're enjoying yourself.

AMY: Be honest. You don't wish it would have been
better received?

CHARLES: Of course I do, who wouldn't wish that—

AMY: And you don't want to go on MSNBC to meet Rachel Maddow.

CHARLES: Are you insane?! Of course I want to meet Rachel Maddow!

AMY: So do I! That's a normal thing to want! What's not normal is playing nice with neo-Nazis and Klansmen for press.

CHARLES: You think this is about press?!

AMY: *(Over him)* Otherwise, and on some level I know you know this, you might find yourself on MSNBC for entirely the wrong reasons.

CHARLES: My reasons are pure. Don't you worry about that. "Press." Really…Amy…that's rich.

(A knock on the door)

CHARLES: Come in!

(BAXTER enters.)

BAXTER: Charles!

CHARLES: Hey, look at this!

BAXTER: Man of the hour!

CHARLES: Oh, God…don't…

BAXTER: Ah, bring it on in here you Nazi-sympathizing son-of-a…

(CHARLES and BAXTER share a warm embrace.)

CHARLES: *(Tone growing serious)* Hey…how are you?

BAXTER: Okay, okay.

CHARLES: You holding up?

BAXTER: I'm doing okay.

CHARLES: You got my letter?

BAXTER: Yes. And thank you.

CHARLES: Amy, you remember Baxter Forrest.

AMY: Yes, of course. Hi.

BAXTER: Dean Katz, how've you been?

AMY: I'm all right. And…Amy, please. *(Sad, knowing)* I was, ah…sorry to hear about your father. Charles told me about the beautiful service.

BAXTER: Yeah. Thanks, thank you. I was in town for that, now I'm back to handle his house, pack it up.

AMY: That's tough. I'm sorry. Where was he…?

BAXTER: Roxbury. The house I grew up in.

AMY: That's hard.

BAXTER: Yeah, I mean—I planned to be here a week, but as soon as I got into it…I don't see how I can be here less than a month.

CHARLES: It's one of those things, throw money at it, hire some people to box it up.

BAXTER: I don't know.

CHARLES: I have a great company. Packed up the house when Diane moved out.

BAXTER: You know, I think I want to do it. Be in there. Be there. My cousin's flying in tomorrow, he's gonna give me a hand.

AMY: Well, a week turns into a month, a month turns into two…maybe we can convince you to stay.

BAXTER: Hey, now.

CHARLES: Wouldn't he be great here?

AMY: I'm planting the seed.

CHARLES: *(To* BAXTER*)* You have to actually teach, though. Can't just be a TV pundit.

BAXTER: Oh, then I'm out.

(They all laugh, good-naturedly.)

CHARLES: Nice to picture, isn't it? Conquering student returns home…

BAXTER: I'm loving UChicago.

CHARLES: Oh sure, great place.

AMY: Is Pat Moran still there?

BAXTER: You bet. Chair of the department now.

(AMY's *cell phone rings. She eyes the screen.*)

AMY: I have to take this. (*Answers, nervous; into phone*) Hello… Hi, yes… They *did*, all right… Yes, I'll run home to pick Eliot up and we'll, ah, we can be at the office in, say, forty minutes?… Right… Great, thanks… Thank you. (*Ends the call; to* BAXTER) Good to see you. Congratulations on all your recent success. Sorry again about your father.

BAXTER: Thank you.

(CHARLES *steps to* AMY, *places a hand gently on her arm.*)

CHARLES: Good luck.

AMY: (*Nods thanks; then*) We're not done. I'm calling you after your class, if the students haven't murdered you by then. Which, come to think of it…problem solved. (*She exits.*)

BAXTER: She all right?

CHARLES: Her husband. Prostate cancer.

BAXTER: Ah, shit.

(*More chants rise from below outside.*)

BAXTER: Lot going on.

CHARLES: Yeah.

(BAXTER *sees the sailboat model.*)

BAXTER: There it is. The legend. Looks good. Been working on it?

CHARLES: There's always something.

BAXTER: What about, are you still assistant-coaching the sailing team?

CHARLES: I'm not. Didn't have as much time, and I've had a knee thing. Plus, honestly, last year with the divorce…

BAXTER: I get it.

CHARLES: Miss it, though.

BAXTER: And how've, um…how've you been doing with…do you and Diane talk much?

CHARLES: Very rarely. It's phenomenal. (Pause) You know, truly, it was a beautiful service. The pastor… so powerful. And that crowd. If you gotta go—and I'm not saying he did, of course—you want your funeral packed to the rafters. There's a man who mattered to people.

BAXTER: I was glad you could be there.

CHARLES: Wouldn't have missed it.

(Beat)

BAXTER: So. You want to talk about this piece of shit you invited to campus?

CHARLES: Happily.

BAXTER: Because you're able to do this, I know you are—to step back and look at what this looks like.

CHARLES: No, I see it: he comes to campus—and this is what the plan is, I'm not going into this blind—he looks like a racist clown. He doesn't come, I rescind the invite, it looks like we're scared of open debate, opposed to free speech—

BAXTER: It wouldn't look like you're opposed to free speech! It would look like you're discerning about who you invite to speak freely here.

CHARLES: So, censorship.

BAXTER: You're not the government. You run a lecture series at a private university.

CHARLES: I'm aware of the distinction.

BAXTER: So, you agree this is a *choice*, that you aren't *bound* to—

CHARLES: Wait, but—so, you're saying—

BAXTER: What I'm saying is, I think…I think you should disinvite him. Today. Today'd be good.

CHARLES: I've always gone with my gut. And this time my gut says Carver and his people would view a pulled invite as a victory.

BAXTER: Not as big a victory as giving a lecture at Harvard.

CHARLES: Oh, I'm—coffee? Anything to drink? I'm sorry, I should've offered sooner.

BAXTER: I'm good, thanks.

(CHARLES *crosses, refills his own coffee mug.*)

BAXTER: We need barriers to entry. Barriers to entry *in the discourse.* If you believe certain things, good for you, but you do not get invited to the table where the grown-ups are talking.

CHARLES: Well—but I'm—you have to commit, to—as I have all my life—to being a free speech absolutist.

BAXTER: Do I? The Paradox of Tolerance.

CHARLES: Popper, yes. You think that's where we are?

BAXTER: A society's infinite tolerance of open intolerance leads to one place only: the destruction of that society.

CHARLES: I still have faith in the strength of institutions.

BAXTER: Good luck with that. The way I see it, especially now, life is too short and the stakes are too high to engage with the holders of certain viewpoints. *(Rattling off his list)* Creationists, Holocaust deniers, Klansmen, Yankee fans.

CHARLES: The answer to hate speech is more speech.

BAXTER: The answer to Nazis is pipes and bats.

CHARLES: You joined Antifa out in Chicago?

BAXTER: Now, *there's* an idea.

CHARLES: Of a sort. But, what's the *real* answer?

BAXTER: I don't know. *(Pause)* But I do know this. I love watching videos of Nazis getting punched.

CHARLES: Violence is wrong, but I love those, too.

BAXTER: Love 'em. It's just good content.

(The door flies open. LUCAS enters in a rush, but stops on a dime when he sees CHARLES and BAXTER talking. LUCAS' gaming headset is strapped onto his shoulder bag.)

LUCAS: Whoop, sorry! *(Without ever taking his hand off the doorknob, he exits and slams the door behind him.)*

CHARLES: One second, Lucas!

LUCAS: *(Offstage)* Not a problem! It was wrong to barge in and for that I apologize!

BAXTER: *(Quiet)* One of your Ph.Ds?

CHARLES: Yes.

BAXTER: Good?

(CHARLES nods "yes".)

BAXTER: He apply for the fellowship?

CHARLES: He did.

BAXTER: And?

CHARLES: Strong contender.

BAXTER: "Strong contender." Okay! *(He checks the time on his phone.)* I gotta run.

CHARLES: Wait, hang on…just… *(Vulnerable)* Did you see the op-ed in the *Globe*?

BAXTER: I saw it on Twitter, yeah.

CHARLES: And?

BAXTER: That's not you.

CHARLES: Thank you. It's not. And people *know* that…

BAXTER: I know that's not you.

CHARLES: I hate hatred.

BAXTER: *(Pause)* That's good.

CHARLES: Book that made my career was about Freedom Summer.

BAXTER: *The Boys in the Car* is a classic. No question. But this… *(Considers how to say it)* With Carver, the symposium… *(Pause)* You built this from the ground up for thirteen years!

CHARLES: Fifteen.

BAXTER: Fifteen. You crafted it year in, year out, with care. *(Nods to the boat model)* You tend to do that. *(Pause)* And now…after you built this robust, real thing…you want to hand a jackhammer to some Klansman with a hundred-dollar haircut.

CHARLES: These people—Carver, and the others—they think they're intellectuals—

BAXTER: They're not.

CHARLES: Exactly. EXACTLY. Who better to show them that than us?

(Beat)

*(*BAXTER *regards his old teacher, his friend.)*

BAXTER: I'm gonna head out, see Jameelah before her class.

CHARLES: Oh. I didn't know you knew her.

BAXTER: Met a few times. And we've done the talking head boxes together on CNN.

CHARLES: That's right. Sure. (*He crosses to the office door.*)

BAXTER: But I'm gonna text you. I want to keep talking about this. You still have time.

CHARLES: To change course.

BAXTER: (*Re: chants outside*) I mean, Jesus, Charles. Listen to that.

CHARLES: If you need any help at the house—anything at all—call me and I'm there.

BAXTER: Thank you.

CHARLES: I am incredibly proud of you.

(*A moment of genuine connection between* CHARLES *and* BAXTER.)

(CHARLES *opens the door.* LUCAS *is on the other side, clearly contrite.*)

CHARLES: Lucas.

LUCAS: I am so sorry. Extremely rude.

CHARLES: This is Baxter Forrest.

LUCAS: Hello.

BAXTER: Pleased to meet you.

(LUCAS' *phone rings in his pocket. He slides it out to look at the screen. Seeing the number, he is distracted.*)

CHARLES: (*To* LUCAS) Are we keeping you from something?

(LUCAS *silences the phone.*)

LUCAS: No! Sorry. *(Pockets the phone)* Sorry. Do you know who leaked the list?

CHARLES: No.

BAXTER: *(Leaving)* Okay. I'm texting you.

(As BAXTER goes, he bumps into MAGGIE, who is entering.)

MAGGIE: Oh!

BAXTER: Pardon me.

MAGGIE: No, it's my fault.

BAXTER: *(Extends hand)* I'm Baxter.

MAGGIE: I know. Maggie.

BAXTER: Hi, Maggie. Excuse me. *(He exits.)*

MAGGIE: That was pretty cool. Hi. So—do you know who leaked the list?

CHARLES: Dean Katz's office is looking into it.

MAGGIE: Well. I just came to see how you're doing.

LUCAS: Me, too. Just checking in.

CHARLES: "Just checking in." Not just…checking in to see about the fellowship.

MAGGIE: What?

CHARLES: See if the committee has reached a decision.

LUCAS: No. What?

CHARLES: The decision has not been made. But soon. I know it's hard. Have you heard from anywhere else yet?

LUCAS: I did *not* get Wash U. Or Minnesota, I heard they were looking for diversity.

CHARLES: Maggie?

MAGGIE: UC Davis. Someone updated the wiki today. Interviews have been scheduled, just not for me.

CHARLES: It's okay. Only need one.

MAGGIE: It's fine. It'll be fine. I actually, ah, came with an offer for you. An invitation. As you know—and as you can literally hear at this moment—the students are upset. *(Pause)* I know you, what's in your heart—I knew why you were doing this—when you told us—

CHARLES: Free speech. Rigorous open debate.

LUCAS: Right.

MAGGIE: Right. But the kids…they don't know that, or know you as well, so the shock of this has triggered them.

CHARLES: They have been "triggered".

MAGGIE: Yes. And were he to come here—Carver— to this campus—they feel—not me—but they feel, because I've spoken to many of them, and they are *good kids,* they really are—they feel his words would cause lasting wounds.

LUCAS: Words would "wound them"?

(CHARLES' *cell phone rings. He looks at the screen.)*

CHARLES: *(To* LUCAS *and* MAGGIE*)* Excuse me. *(Answers; into phone)* Hello…

(CHARLES *steps off to the side by the boat model to take the call.* LUCAS *and* MAGGIE *step downstage to speak hushed, out of earshot of* CHARLES, *who is inaudible on the phone.)*

LUCAS: You're really on the side of these hysterics. These *children.*

MAGGIE: Coming from a guy who plays video games all night, to the point where he nods off all day.

LUCAS: I have. Sleep apnea.

MAGGIE: You showed up to teach a class still wearing your gaming headset.

LUCAS: Honest mistake.

MAGGIE: Twice. You did that *twice*.

LUCAS: Video games are interactive narratives for all ages.

MAGGIE: Maybe if they made an "interactive narrative" about beet farming in seventeenth-century Sweden you would finish your dissertation.

LUCAS: I am almost done! Besides, I didn't need it finished to be his research assistant last summer.

MAGGIE: No, but he approved my undergraduate seminar because he knew I *was* finished.

LUCAS: Of *course* you're finished, how much is there to say about a gaggle of bisexual suffragettes running a boarding house in Saratoga Springs.

(*They eye each other.*)

(CHARLES *ends his call, steps back over.*)

CHARLES: What were we saying?

LUCAS: That words can wound.

MAGGIE: I'm just here as a voice for the students. They feel—again, not me—but these kids feel threatened by Carver's speech.

CHARLES: He will not be permitted to come here and make threats.

MAGGIE: Just that he is speaking, that would be the threat.

CHARLES: That's not how threats work.

LUCAS: Or words.

MAGGIE: (*Ignoring* LUCAS; *to* CHARLES) So, I want to invite you—and obviously this has been thrown together last minute, it's sort of a developing story type situation, obviously—this afternoon—I've been speaking since last night, since the list came out, with some of the students from Hillel. They, in partnership with the BSA, they're inviting you to join them this afternoon to discuss the list at an SSM.

CHARLES: "SSM"?

MAGGIE: Sorry—Safe Space Meet.

CHARLES: "Safe Space Meet."

MAGGIE: It's a meeting…that is…safe.

(Beat)

(CHARLES *hangs his head.)*

MAGGIE: They want to have a dialogue—

CHARLES: No.

MAGGIE: Professor Nichols—

CHARLES: No, Maggie. I won't go to it. I won't be subjected to a tribunal of triggered children. Besides, I'll be gone this afternoon. And if you two are interested, so will you. *(Pause for effect)* That was Carver on the phone. He wants to meet.

LUCAS: Like a Safe Space Meet? Sorry.

MAGGIE: Where? Here?

CHARLES: No. He's traveling now. Called from Maine. He wants it to be there, at the house of one of his supporters.

LUCAS: Why does he want to meet?

CHARLES: He said…to feel me out. See if I can be trusted.

MAGGIE: If *you* can be trusted…

CHARLES: I'd love it if you both came with.

MAGGIE: Are you serious?

CHARLES: He won't be alone. Why should I be? You can both take notes. I mean, we all can.

(LUCAS *and* MAGGIE *exchange a look. Both unsure. It's clear that this is unusual.*)

CHARLES: We can't allow our…well, our personal aversions to a subject's viewpoint to, to prevent us from seeing—really seeing—that subject up close. *(Pause)* All right. Full disclosure? All right. I need someone with me—in case this becomes public before it's meant to. *(Indicates out window)* As can happen. If Carver, if he misrepresents something I say—

LUCAS: You want backup.

CHARLES: If it turns into a—yes. If it becomes a he-said-he-said.

LUCAS: Makes sense.

CHARLES: I'd offer to drive, to make things easy, but that's not the arrangement. I'm to—we are, if you elect to come—to take a train up to Saco where I—where we—will be picked up and driven to the house. Actually, he called it a compound.

LUCAS: They won't give you an address?

CHARLES: No.

LUCAS: Huh. Well. I'll go.

(CHARLES *and* LUCAS *look to* MAGGIE.)

MAGGIE: I'm sorry, but I—no. I can't.

CHARLES: It's entirely your choice.

MAGGIE: *(Pause)* Maybe this isn't my place, but—don't fall into their trap.

CHARLES: "Their trap."

MAGGIE: I think this whole thing is a trap.

LUCAS: "It's a trap!" *(Pause) Star Wars. (Tries again)* "It's a trap!"

CHARLES: *(To* MAGGIE*)* This could be very interesting. Fascinating field research. Think of it like a day sail.

MAGGIE: "Sailing with the Klan." Okay, I thought about it.

CHARLES: Really—it's why people set out for the day. You go somewhere, reach a point, experience a thing…you have a different view on the way home. Perspective.

MAGGIE: I don't sit down with White supremacists. That's not what you do with White supremacists.

CHARLES: We'll be safe.

MAGGIE: I don't feel safe. I *wouldn't*. Carver's father was a Grand Wizard. He thinks no one died in the gas chambers. That, what, my great aunt and uncle stepped on rusty nails at Treblinka?

CHARLES: He is a monster. The campaign to discredit him—and people like him—must be sustained, peaceful, and conducted at close range.

MAGGIE: Well. Face to face is too close for me.

LUCAS: The answer to hate speech is more speech.

MAGGIE: You don't have to worry, it doesn't affect you! *(To* CHARLES*)* No offense, or you. It'll be people like me on the trains.

CHARLES: There won't be any trains!

LUCAS: *("Actually…")* We're taking a train today.

(MAGGIE *levels a look at* LUCAS*.)*

CHARLES: I have a class to teach.

(LUCAS *and* MAGGIE *know that's their cue to go.)*

MAGGIE: *(Hail Mary)* We can move the meeting—to talk about this—to another time, both groups are open to it, if you change your mind.

CHARLES: I won't. But if you change yours—Lucas and I will be on the 2:20 out of North Station. (*To* LUCAS) We'll meet for a drink at 1:30. Good?

LUCAS: Great.

(*As* LUCAS *and* MAGGIE *reach the door, the chants outside grow in ferocity and volume.*)

CHARLES: There are twice as many of them now. Am I gonna have to sneak out the back?

MAGGIE: They're out back, too.

CHARLES: I may need a disguise.

LUCAS: Try a hood?

(CHARLES *and* MAGGIE *look at him disapprovingly.*)

LUCAS: I'm sorry, I legitimately don't know what's wrong with me sometimes.

CHARLES: Goodbye.

(LUCAS *and* MAGGIE *exit.*)

(CHARLES *inches to the wall and carefully peers out at the protestors.*)

(*Then* CHARLES *notices something on the sailboat model. He steps over to the case, opens the glass, and delicately adjusts a minor detail.*)

(*Lights down*)

Scene Three

(*Lights up on the platform of a small train station. A bench. A stopped train is offstage.*)

(CHARLES *and* LUCAS *hold cups of Amtrak coffee.*)

(*A mounted speaker crackles to life.*)

LOUDSPEAKER VOICE: Thank you for your patience, folks. Should only be another few minutes here as we take a look at the issue.

CHARLES: "Another few minutes."

LUCAS: That patented Amtrak optimism.

CHARLES: *(Pause)* After I turned ten, my parents used to put me on the train by myself once a summer, up to visit cousins in Cumberland.

LUCAS: That's young to travel solo.

CHARLES: I loved it. You can't do things like that anymore. *(He takes a sip of his coffee.)* You know, I think that one's mine.

LUCAS: Oh—really?

CHARLES: When we were getting up from the seats, I must've grabbed the wrong one.

LUCAS: Here, no problem.

(CHARLES *and* LUCAS *switch coffee cups, take sips.)*

(Beat)

LUCAS: This is ironic.

CHARLES: What's that.

LUCAS: We're on our way to see a man who aligns with neo-Nazis. Who says the Holocaust didn't happen. And here we are…on a train platform…

CHARLES: Oh, Lucas.

LUCAS: I'm sorry, that's wildly inappropriate.

CHARLES: Really.

LUCAS: I don't know why I say things sometimes! My mouth is just…

CHARLES: Well, whatever put that in your head, put it out.

LUCAS: It's out, it's out.

(CHARLES *sits on the bench, rubs his aching knee.*)

LUCAS: We could use one of Frank's jokes to clear the air.

CHARLES: So, you're a regular there. If you know Frank's comedic stylings.

LUCAS: I don't know about "a regular". But I like that bar.

CHARLES: Frank does love a good joke.

LUCAS: I wouldn't say "good".

CHARLES: No. But he's a fine bartender.

LUCAS: Yeah. Seemed like you two were tight.

CHARLES: I have a…it sounds silly, but…we have a book club.

LUCAS: Stop.

CHARLES: It's true.

LUCAS: That is adorable.

CHARLES: It's actually kind of refreshing.

LUCAS: How'd it start?

CHARLES: It was six or seven months ago. He was really down. Frank's brother and his family had just moved to Nashua.

LUCAS: That's less than an hour's drive.

CHARLES: (*Shrugs*) He needed something social. Consistent.

LUCAS: Look at you. Very kind.

CHARLES: Well. Half my drinks are on the house, so everybody wins.

LUCAS: You guys mostly do beach reads?

CHARLES: No. No "beach reads". History books.

LUCAS: Who picks the books?

CHARLES: I pick them. Frank reads, then we discuss. He's also interested in sailing, grew up on the Cape, so we talk about that sometimes, too. He's working on his first model boat.

LUCAS: Nice. Last week I was in there with some people, Frank comes over, "Listen to this one". He says, "What's purple and hums?"

CHARLES: Oh. I don't know.

LUCAS: An electric grape.

CHARLES: Why does it hum?

LUCAS: Because it doesn't know the words. *(Beat)* And it's impossible to make him stop.

CHARLES: What if it's a green grape?

LUCAS: Exactly.

CHARLES: And what's its power source?

LUCAS: Right. The story's full of holes.

CHARLES: *(Looks off)* Are the repairmen even here?

(CHARLES' *cell phone rings. He looks at the screen, then silences the call.)*

LUCAS: You can—you can take that.

CHARLES: It's fine. It's Baxter.

LUCAS: By all means—I can give you some privacy.

CHARLES: No need. He's just calling to—he's probably just calling to take another shot. He tried to talk me out of coming here.

LUCAS: Ah. Okay.

(CHARLES' *phone dings with an incoming text message. He reads the screen.)*

LUCAS: He's persistent.

CHARLES: One of many strong qualities. He's a good friend.

LUCAS: That's great. I like that. We met before, he forgot. At the Columbia conference last year we met. *(Beat)* How close are you with him?

CHARLES: Close. See him on TV more than I see him in person. But we e-mail and talk.

LUCAS: He's pretty hot right now.

CHARLES: You'll be there someday.

LUCAS: I doubt that.

CHARLES: Don't be negative.

LUCAS: Not negative. I'm not a negative person. I'm just a realist. I'm not…I don't know…of the cultural moment.

(CHARLES *turns to* LUCAS *with a questioning look.)*

LUCAS: I'm not…you know, I'm not… *(He waves his hands broadly over his body.)*

CHARLES: Good at charades?

LUCAS: No, I'm just…I'm just a White guy doing boring work on the agrarian economy and practices of seventeenth-century Sweden.

CHARLES: Your work is less current.

LUCAS: We *are* historians, though.

CHARLES: Well, I should say—

LUCAS: No, I agree. My work has less current relevance.

CHARLES: *(Pause)* I know exactly what you mean.

LUCAS: Like, with Jameelah. She's brilliant.

CHARLES: Yes.

LUCAS: She's everywhere.

CHARLES: The camera loves her.

LUCAS: Right, right. And all off one book.

CHARLES: She's gifted.

LUCAS: Definitely. Definitely. Did you hear she signed a deal with Amazon to teach a course?

CHARLES: What?

LUCAS: With audiobooks. Something. I'm not sure how it works. Didn't you do one of those Great Courses? After *The Boys in the Car*?

CHARLES: I did a few.

(Beat)

LUCAS: Yeah…I don't know, I've just been thinking… how you're always saying, when we're writing, how we need to get into the subjects' heads.

CHARLES: You have to do it.

LUCAS: To look at what they looked at, try to picture how they saw the events.

CHARLES: That's the difference-maker.

LUCAS: Right. So I've been thinking about Carver. And wondering…how does he see this?

CHARLES: How does he see what?

LUCAS: This cultural moment. When he sees Baxter on TV, sees Jameelah on TV, their books written about, you turn on NPR…

CHARLES: I don't think Carver listens to a lot of NPR.

LUCAS: Fair.

CHARLES: Hard to picture him carrying a tote bag at a torch rally.

LUCAS: Yeah.

CHARLES: Driving a replica Panzer tank, listening to Terry Gross.

LUCAS: Yeah, no. But did I…you know what, I feel like I framed the question poorly.

CHARLES: No, I see what you're asking. I don't know. What does Carver see when he looks at someone like Jameelah…? Because this is less Baxter than Jameelah, just to be clear.

LUCAS: Sure.

CHARLES: I think if you asked Carver…and maybe tonight I will…he'd likely say she's being held to a different—but I'm, I'm only saying this, you're asking me…as an intellectual exercise…

LUCAS: Of course, I'm—

CHARLES: A thought experiment.

LUCAS: An exercise. I know.

CHARLES: Because I understand American Nazis. I mean come on, I wrote a book about them.

LUCAS: I'd call it *the* book, but…all right.

CHARLES: *(Over him)* So, I know, that sickness, from the `20s and `30s, it's never really gone away. Carver's sick with it now. And you're asking, how does he see all this? Well. Through his eyes, there might appear to be a different set of standards applied to Jameelah and to certain other scholars, commentators, what have you.

LUCAS: How so? I mean, that's interesting, but how do you mean?

CHARLES: Well, with her book, which is something of a slim volume—and I just don't see her as much of a historian. Baxter is different.

LUCAS: Right. He had a better teacher.

CHARLES: That's not—thank you, but—that's not what I meant.

LUCAS: No…

CHARLES: I mean, the way she manages scope—for a cultural microhistory—

LUCAS: Yes. I see.

CHARLES: And Jameelah, this book…as best I understand it…and I did read it, but I read it quickly… the point of the book, well, first of all, the literal title is *Against Whiteness*.

LUCAS: Not subtle—but don't, don't get me wrong, I like it! It's bold.

CHARLES: And this argument she makes, that Whiteness is only absence, "the absence of", seems reductive, and flashy, and bankrupt.

LUCAS: *(Pause)* And this is *Carver* saying this.

CHARLES: That's, yes, that's what I think would "trigger" him, to use the sad vernacular of the day, the total negation of the system that has propped him up his whole life, his White life, he feels under siege.

LUCAS: I think that's right.

CHARLES: Whiteness under siege. "The White man is evil, the White man is responsible for all ills." I mean, all right, to a point, but…

(The mounted speaker crackles to life.)

LOUDSPEAKER VOICE: Attention please, the yellow parking spaces are permit-only, so if you're the driver of the, uh, the green Subaru Outback please move your vehicle to a metered spot, thank you.

(Beat)

LUCAS: Her larger point, it seems to me, is about culture. That White *culture*—

CHARLES: Again, I read it quickly.

LUCAS: She's saying White culture is the *absence* of culture.

CHARLES: Which is patently absurd. Just from a historical standpoint.

LUCAS: That's one area of agreement between you and the White Identitarians.

CHARLES: The only point, I'm sure. But you don't have to be a White nationalist to realize that an Irishman's culture is different from an Italian-American's; is different from a Swedish farmer's; is different from a Jewish lawyer's in New York.

LUCAS: Right, right. Not that Carver would concede that Jews are White, but—

CHARLES: Good point. But other than that—

LUCAS: Yes. But to the question of "whiteness" and what it means to Carver…

CHARLES: In Carver's head it's all related to the concept of "White pride". Because at question is the very *notion* of pride, when they consume the media—which *does* tend to skew liberal, thank goodness—what Carver and his people hear is, "Stop feeling pride, you have nothing of which to be proud". The backlash…is not a surprise. As a White man, I am not ensnared by any of it…but more foolish people, people less fortunate…to them, Carver's rhetoric has appeal.

LUCAS: Are you proud to be White?

CHARLES: I'm not proud "to be White", no. I'm proud to simply *be*. To be a professor, a writer, proud to be of my family, five generations at Harvard—

LUCAS: That's not nothing.

CHARLES: Hundreds of years my family has been in this country. Escaped an England that would have strung them up or cut their throats. For what? For a slightly different worship of God. I'm proud of that. Not Whiteness.

LUCAS: Makes sense.

CHARLES: You're White.

LUCAS: *(Pause)* Yes.

CHARLES: Are you proud?

LUCAS: I don't know…*can* you be proud to be White?

CHARLES: Of course. Of course you *can*, but—

LUCAS: People are free to, of course—in America—

CHARLES: *(Dry)* There's a precedent, certainly.

LUCAS: So, while one *can*…

CHARLES: But look, I don't want to come off as if *I* believe that.

LUCAS: Certainly not, no.

CHARLES: That's Carver, that reasoning, what I was putting forth, that's a White nationalist mindset.

LUCAS: Right.

CHARLES: I *want* diversity.

LUCAS: Of course!

CHARLES: Many seats at the table.

LUCAS: A big table.

CHARLES: Yes.

(Beat)

LUCAS: I think you're right, though, on free speech grounds. That he should come to campus. That his ideas should be well-lit and subject to inspection.

CHARLES: We have to allow it.

LUCAS: Because we have the power, and in terms of access, of standing, comparatively, they have so much less.

CHARLES: There's a nautical law for that.

LUCAS: You have a nautical law for everything.

CHARLES: That a vessel under power of motor must grant right of way to a vessel under power of sail.

LUCAS: Huh. *(Pause)* I just want to say thank you. You've done a lot for me. You're doing a lot for me now.

CHARLES: You're welcome.

LUCAS: No matter what happens with the fellowship.

(The mounted speaker crackles to life.)

LOUDSPEAKER VOICE: Uh, thank you ladies and gentlemen, I have an update. Technicians are at work on the, uh, the problem. We're lookin at about another forty-five minutes. We'll have you back on your way soon as we can, thank you.

LUCAS: Amtrak: we may not get you there on time, and also we just may not get you there.

CHARLES: We'll be fine. We'll have another coffee.

LUCAS: I think I'd like it your way this time.

(CHARLES looks at LUCAS. LUCAS smiles.)

LUCAS: It's okay. I don't judge. I could smell the whiskey, when we switched cups before.

CHARLES: I can pour us a drink. Bottle's in my briefcase.

LUCAS: Thanks.

CHARLES: You do seem nervous.

LUCAS: Do I? I don't know. Meeting Carver…

CHARLES: Don't be nervous. He'll like it if you are.

LUCAS: Okay.

CHARLES: Don't give him that.

LUCAS: I'll try.

CHARLES: Remember. We have what he wants.

(CHARLES *hands* LUCAS *his coffee cup.*)

CHARLES: Drink this.

(LUCAS *downs what's left in one gulp.*)

CHARLES: Better?

LUCAS: It's a start.

CHARLES: Good. Let's talk about something else.

LUCAS: Okay.

CHARLES: Want to hear a joke?

LUCAS: This one of Frank's?

CHARLES: Have you heard the one about the pirate?

(*Lights down*)

Scene Five

(*In the dimmest light. The entryway of a home. Late at night. Partially packed moving boxes all around, many of which are stuffed with math books of various kinds: textbooks, research and theory volumes, journals. Semi-organized stacks of them are visible in the room off the entryway. Some are stacked on the bench in the entryway itself.*)

(*Knocking on the door. The knocking turns to pounding. A switch is flipped. Lights come up.*)

(*BAXTER enters. He opens the door to reveal CHARLES standing there, harried.*)

CHARLES: Thank you, thank you.

BAXTER: Come in, Charlie. Jesus.

CHARLES: Thank you, Bax.

BAXTER: Mm-hm. (*He looks outside, quickly scanning, before closing the door.*)

CHARLES: Thank you. Thank you…

BAXTER: Stop saying that.

CHARLES: Now you've seen it. You've read about what happened.

BAXTER: It's all over Twitter, it's everywhere.

CHARLES: She's…are there any updates?

BAXTER: Just, she's, the latest says she's still in surgery. Were you at the hospital?

CHARLES: No.

BAXTER: Where was she shot? There's a lot of conflicting information.

CHARLES: The chest. A lung? I don't, I don't know…

(BAXTER *helps* CHARLES *take a seat on the bench.*)

BAXTER: Okay…settle down…

(CHARLES' *attention is drawn to a stack of math books on the bench. He picks one up and thumbs through it.*)

CHARLES: Bet he wished you'd gone into math.

BAXTER: He didn't.

CHARLES: Generations of kids…he mattered to people. I was never much good with numbers. (*Re: books*) What'll you do with them all?

BAXTER: His department at the high school set up a, ah…they set up some local donations. Are you… Charles, look at me. Are you okay?

(CHARLES *sets the book down, then looks up at* BAXTER.)

CHARLES: I could use a drink.

BAXTER: I think you're good.

CHARLES: Come on.

BAXTER: Smell like you're a few deep.

CHARLES: I'm fine. I drove.

BAXTER: I noticed.

CHARLES: Bax, please.

BAXTER: Not a good idea.

CHARLES: Goddammit, I'm not a child!

BAXTER: I won't serve you a drink, Charlie. This is my father's house.

CHARLES: What does that mean? "Your father's house." Yes. It is. Yes.

(Beat)

BAXTER: You can sober up here, but you can't stay.

CHARLES: I don't want to stay, I want…

BAXTER: What do you want? Tell me. Tell me what you want.

(CHARLES *eyes* BAXTER.)

CHARLES: What's her status now?

(BAXTER *scrolls on his phone, reads.)*

BAXTER: No news.

CHARLES: How many are there?

BAXTER: How many what?

CHARLES: Students. In the waiting area. Tweeting updates.

BAXTER: They're not updating a head count. How many were at the compound?

CHARLES: Thirty. Forty. Hard to say. How did they get the address? How did they find the address?

BAXTER: These Nazis are attention whores. Protests are good for them. Violence is better. Somebody *leaked* the address.

CHARLES: If they hadn't—

BAXTER: But they did. *(Beat)* Listen. Stay here until it's safe for you to get behind the wheel. I'm not playing. Grab a shower, brew some coffee, whatever you need to do. Then let yourself out. I have to get to sleep.

CHARLES: Wait—hey. What?

BAXTER: What's the problem?

CHARLES: "The problem" is, you're, you're treating me like I'm a stranger. And it feels like—

BAXTER: I have shit to do in the morning. Hours at a law firm. Pick my cousin up at Logan. I have to sleep.

CHARLES: Bax, hang on—I need you—

BAXTER: "You need me."

CHARLES: I need your help, but you're acting like—

BAXTER: What could I possibly help with?

CHARLES: You're acting like I, what, like I did this? That this is—that I shot her—

BAXTER: You didn't shoot her.

CHARLES: Okay! So we agree I didn't shoot anybody!

BAXTER: But she was shot. Outside the compound. Where you went to break bread with a White nationalist.

CHARLES: That's—

BAXTER: A young woman was shot. A young Black woman was shot. A student. With a name. Jessica Matthews.

CHARLES: I know what it looks like—

BAXTER: You're in trouble, Charlie.

CHARLES: I know that. You think I don't fucking know that.

BAXTER: It's worse than you think. Than you realize, is what I'm saying.

CHARLES: But she's gonna live—

BAXTER: You'd better hope so.

CHARLES: She *will.* She *will* live, and that's a good thing, this—this will all be—it's what makes these people monsters, these vile—these, these pigs.

BAXTER: Look at me. Stop. Stop. Look at me. You're drunk. You're not processing this. I understand. I understand that. But I will not care for you tonight.

CHARLES: Bax…

BAXTER: There is a young woman on an operating table in Maine, some hospital she's never seen, in a room where she may never wake up. That's you. That's on you.

CHARLES: I didn't—I didn't shoot her—the kids showed up.

BAXTER: You led them there.

CHARLES: I did not. They went to protest.

BAXTER: *You.* They went to protest *you.*

(Beat)

CHARLES: It went to shit. In the middle of dinner. I have no idea what happened.

BAXTER: Charles.

CHARLES: We're eating, and then, just…Carver, he, he *turns*…something *turned* in the guy.

BAXTER: I don't give a shit.

CHARLES: They usher us out. Fast. All of a sudden it's as if, if, like some *wire* had been tripped.

BAXTER: I don't want to hear it.

CHARLES: It couldn't have been the protestors showing up at the gate, that was earlier—

BAXTER: SHUT UP. SHUT UP. Goddammit I am really on the edge with you. I am fucking on it. Why are you here? Why did you come here?

(*Beat*)

(CHARLES *crosses to a stack of moving boxes. He eyes some of the books inside, then looks around, taking in the room.*)

CHARLES: My house is empty like this…looks half moved-out…I haven't replaced what she took, the, the furniture, when she left, Diane—

BAXTER: You're gonna answer me. Right now. What do you want?

CHARLES: (*Pause*) If you could help me. Please. Help me with writing something.

BAXTER: You want to write something.

CHARLES: Not me. You.

(BAXTER, *unblinking, stares at* CHARLES.)

CHARLES: For *you* to write something. A statement.

BAXTER: "A statement." About what?

CHARLES: Me. About me.

BAXTER: What about you? What is my statement to be about?

CHARLES: That I'm—come on—that I'm a good person, a defender of—that I'm an ally.

BAXTER: "You're an ally."

CHARLES: Well, am I not? Would you not say that—

BAXTER: No.

CHARLES: "No."

BAXTER: No.

CHARLES: "No" you will not write it, or "no" I'm not an ally?

BAXTER: Both.

CHARLES: Well, that's—that's just bullshit. It's bullshit. What? Because I am. I *am* one. And it would really help me, for you to do something. On Facebook, or Twitter—something that could get out there—

BAXTER: Yeah, I'm not doing that.

CHARLES: You ingrate. I found you. I plucked you out. I cleaned you up.

BAXTER: Say again? You "cleaned me up"?

CHARLES: Dammit, you could help me here.

BAXTER: I can't do it.

CHARLES: Well, why not? Why the fuck not?

BAXTER: Because you have bad judgement. Because you erred in this. Because you are a bad judge of character.

CHARLES: Even though I judge yours highly? You're supposed to be my friend.

BAXTER: I know.

CHARLES: We go back. You know me. I know you.

BAXTER: You don't. That's it. That's exactly it. You don't, you never have. You don't see the people around you. Not really. Not who they really are, *what* they are. You see them as role-players, as guests—cast in the dinner parties that are your seminars. You've always cast those rooms to suit your moods and feed your ego. I know. I know your dinner parties as well as anyone because you once cast me.

CHARLES: Why haven't you ever said anything?

BAXTER: It's rude to insult the host.

CHARLES: You knew what you were doing.

BAXTER: Of course I did. I know what I was in your eyes. I know what role I played. I chose to play it because I knew it would put me on a path. And I knew where that path would take me. So I walked it. I walked it. I did that. But it meant always holding something back from you. *(Pause)* It really was a useful fellowship. But what you've done now, here, with Carver, this "free speech" bullshit—and it's bullshit, full stop—"First Amendment" my fuckin ass. All of it has filled me with a deep and abiding regret. I tried to talk to you, Charlie. I tried to help you, to steer you away from this. You are my life's most narcissistic man.

(CHARLES *is beginning to break.)*

CHARLES: Your book is brilliant. It is, it really is.

BAXTER: Charles.

CHARLES: You were good on Bill Maher. Really gave it to him.

BAXTER: Okay, Charles.

(CHARLES *is in his own world, lost.)*

CHARLES: I'm out, I'm, it's been…years now…she's eclipsing me.

BAXTER: "She"?

CHARLES: I'm getting eclipsed in my own department.

BAXTER: Ah. There it is.

CHARLES: I thought this would help. With Carver. I did. Thought it would get things cracking again.

(CHARLES' *phone rings. He silences it. It dings with incoming text messages. He ignores them, all of them.)*

(BAXTER *checks his phone. Refreshes his timeline, reads.)*

BAXTER: She's dead.

CHARLES: What?

BAXTER: Jessica Matthews is dead.

(Lights down)

Scene Six

(Lights up on CHARLES' *office. There are no loud protestors outside.)*

*(*CHARLES *looks exhausted. He has not slept. Cell phone pressed to his ear, he is leaving a voicemail.)*

CHARLES: *(Into phone)* Yeah, hi, Amy, it's Charles. Trying you again. Look, ah, I need to, we need to talk. Okay? All morning, I've been…I've written up a statement. Would love to get your eyes on it before we—well, just, just call me. Okay, thanks. Thank you. *(He ends the call.)*

*(*CHARLES *stands before the glass case, lost in thought, nerves on edge, eyes fixed on the model sailboat.)*

*(*CHARLES' *cell phone rings. He is hopeful that it's* AMY. *Though it isn't her, a kind of relief washes over his face when he sees who is calling.)*

CHARLES: *(Answers; into phone)* Diane, hi… How do you think?… No… Yes… It *is* awful, just a horrible thing… I appreciate you checking in… Yes, but not to the police, to the FBI. They're sending an agent. I'm supposed to… *(Checks the time)* He was supposed to be here twenty minutes ago… Mm-hm, I will. Listen, how, ah, how about you come up for a few days? I can make up the spare room… Mm… Well, just because it might be good to see you, given what's—… No, I understand… No… I, I agree…

(A forceful knock on the door. It startles CHARLES.*)*

CHARLES: *(Into phone)* I have to go, the agent's here…
All right… Thank you… All right. *(He ends the call and
pockets his phone. He crosses to the door. He steels himself,
then opens the door.)*

(Standing there is QUINN.*)*

(Beat)

QUINN: Mr Nichols.

CHARLES: Yes. Yes… Hello.

QUINN: I'm Special Agent Quinn Harris, FBI.

CHARLES: Of course, yes, come in, come in. Please…

*(*CHARLES *stands aside to let* QUINN *enter. He sets out a
chair.)*

CHARLES: Coffee?

QUINN: I'm all set.

CHARLES: *(Gestures to chair)* Would you care to…?

QUINN: *(Sits; looking around)* Thanks. It's quite the
office.

CHARLES: Oh, thank you. I'm here more than I'm home,
so…

*(*CHARLES *takes a pad of paper from his desk, then pulls over
a chair and sits opposite* QUINN, *who readies her notebook
and pen.)*

QUINN: Mr Nichols, I'm with the Joint Terrorism
Task Force out of the Boston Field Office. We are
coordinating the response to the incident because we
handle hate crimes, as well as anything with possible
links to domestic terrorism.

CHARLES: I understand.

QUINN: Thanks for speaking with me this morning.
I know you've had a difficult twenty-four hours.
But before we get into our conversation—which will

primarily entail you walking me through the events of last night—

CHARLES: *(Holds up legal pad)* I made notes.

QUINN: Oh.

CHARLES: So I wouldn't forget anything. Last night, when it was all fresh and clear in my mind.

QUINN: Good thinking. May I have a copy of those when we're done?

CHARLES: Absolutely. They're for you, after all.

QUINN: Great. Now. Before we begin, I have a small confession to make, which—please take in the spirit of full disclosure. I've actually read one of your books.

(CHARLES *is surprised and flattered.*)

CHARLES: *Have* you.

QUINN: In a training seminar. Your book about American Nazi groups in the 1920s and `30s.

CHARLES: I'm honored. To be included, I mean, in the syllabus.

QUINN: An unforgettable book.

CHARLES: Thank you, truly.

QUINN: You're welcome. So. With that out of the way, let's talk about last night.

CHARLES: I am eager to assist however I can. This is an awful, heart-rending tragedy.

QUINN: Yes, it is.

CHARLES: Ms Matthews deserves justice.

QUINN: That's why I'm here. And we can't conduct investigations like this without people like you, people who want to *help*. So, thank you.

CHARLES: Of course. May I ask, if it's permitted…do you have the…have, have you arrested the—

QUINN: We do have the shooter in custody.

CHARLES: That's a relief.

QUINN: I agree. Last night, when you arrived at the compound, what did you see?

(Throughout their conversation QUINN *takes notes. Not constantly, but consistently. When answering,* CHARLES *occasionally consults the notes written on his legal pad.)*

CHARLES: A big gate. There were guards. Armed. Then the long driveway through the woods. I'd estimate it was a quarter-mile. Leading to the main house, where we went inside.

QUINN: Did you visit any of the other buildings on the premises?

CHARLES: No.

QUINN: Okay. Can you describe what took place at the main house?

CHARLES: That's where dinner was served. But first there were cocktails.

QUINN: "Cocktails." All right. And how long would you say you were there—were on the property before the student protestors arrived?

CHARLES: Roughly…one hour. Seventy-five minutes at the most. They were at the gate, outside the main gate. At the other end of the driveway. We couldn't hear them from the house.

QUINN: So, how were you made aware of their presence?

(A knock on the door. It opens. AMY *enters.)*

AMY: Sorry to interrupt.

CHARLES: No, come in. Can she be here?

QUINN: Yes, or we can be alone. It's up to you.

CHARLES: Do we have to be? Legally? Is there—

QUINN: No. It's fine.

CHARLES: She can stay. *(To* AMY*)* You can stay.

*(*AMY *closes the door behind her.)*

CHARLES: *(To* QUINN *re:* AMY*)* This is Dean—

QUINN: We've met. Earlier this morning. *(To* AMY*)* Dean Katz.

AMY: Hello again. Thanks for letting me sit in.

QUINN: *(To* CHARLES*)* Where were we? Yes. The arrival of the student protestors. How were you made aware of their presence?

CHARLES: One of Carver's…I don't know…*assistants* came in and whispered to him. By that time we were eating. This was before the meal was…was broken off. So, after the assistant informed him, Carver looked at us—

QUINN: At you and Lucas Poole.

CHARLES: Yes. He said there were students at the gate.

QUINN: Did he seem bothered?

CHARLES: He seemed amused. Said they were "resourceful". Which I took to mean, that they somehow found the place.

AMY: Carver knows how they found it.

CHARLES: I'm sorry?

AMY: According to the students who were present. The address of the compound was anonymously posted on a message board yesterday afternoon.

QUINN: That's correct. And, Mr Nichols, this is one of the main things I'm trying to figure out…the arrival of the students, the protestors—that is *not* why the dinner was broken off?

CHARLES: No. That happened about…twenty minutes later.

QUINN: Twenty minutes. Okay. And dinner just—Mr Carver just ended it abruptly.

CHARLES: Yes. And we were, we were escorted out.

QUINN: By Mr Carver?

CHARLES: No. The last we saw him was in the dining room. We were taken back to the gate by the same driver who picked us up at the train station in Saco. Never got a name, but he was middle-aged, brown hair…

QUINN: Why did Mr Carver end the dinner?

CHARLES: I don't know. He looked at his phone…

QUINN: His phone.

CHARLES: We were eating. Seven people around the table. And he just…looked at his phone, saw something there, presumably *read* something, *that* I don't know…then he stood up.

QUINN: He stood up. Did he say anything?

CHARLES: No. He looked at me. I asked him what was wrong, but he just walked out.

QUINN: Hm. And said nothing.

CHARLES: His face was red. Flushed. He was angry.

QUINN: And, you say, they "escorted" you out. Was it rough or violent in any way?

CHARLES: No, but it was fast. When the car approached the gate, that's when we first heard them and saw them. There were so many students. Grabbing the gate, shaking it. The car, it couldn't get through, obviously.

QUINN: Why not?

CHARLES: The gate is one of those that opens in the middle. Swings out, both sides. When we pulled up, one of the guards tried to open the gate, but the students blocked it. They pushed against the gate, threw their bodies up against it, straining, really pushing…and the gate wouldn't move. The guards yelled at them to back off, but the students were yelling over them. It was escalating. Lucas and I looked at each other. We didn't know what to do. I saw genuine fear in that young man's eyes. The students would not let that gate open. Then Ms Matthews began to climb the gate. She was shouting. Her fellow students were holding her up.

(AMY *cries silently, wipes away a tear.*)

CHARLES: I heard the gunshot and she fell.

(A long beat)

QUINN: What happened next?

CHARLES: We got out of the car. To help. The gate opened. Students screamed. So many of them screaming. But immediately a few of them loaded her into a car, into the backseat, and drove off.

QUINN: Did you follow?

CHARLES: I wanted to. To the hospital, but—the students were upset. Those who remained spit on us, Lucas and me. A few began striking us. I understand. The driver got us into the safety of his car. He drove us home.

QUINN: Back to Boston.

CHARLES: Yes. The trains don't run that late. The plan was always to be driven back to Boston.

(QUINN *makes notes.*)

CHARLES: Have you spoken to Lucas?

QUINN: We're speaking with him now.

CHARLES: Good. Well. As I said, Ms Matthews deserves justice, swift justice, and I hope I've been able, in some small way, to help clarify events—

QUINN: Couple more things. Then I'll get out of your hair.

CHARLES: *(Pause)* Please.

QUINN: I'm aware that Dean Katz knew Ms Matthews. Did you?

CHARLES: I, ahm…no. *(To* AMY*)* You did?

AMY: She took my seminar.

CHARLES: Oh, Amy…

AMY: Two years ago.

CHARLES: That must be…I'm sorry, that must make this so much more difficult for you.

AMY: Not nearly as difficult as it is for her family. I spoke to them this morning.

CHARLES: Of course. Of course.

QUINN: *(To* CHARLES*)* Here's another thing I'm curious about. And I'm asking because, just looking at it from the outside, a man like him and a respected author like yourself, a professor at Harvard…it's a curious pairing. How did you and Benjamin Carver first come into contact?

CHARLES: Well…for a few years now, he, ahm…he has been making overtures to some of us in the field, leading figures—it's not just me—hoping to come to campus, to campuses…

QUINN: What kind of overtures?

CHARLES: Pitching speech topics, proposing panels and events.

QUINN: Did you ever respond?

CHARLES: Only to say no.

QUINN: Until this year.

CHARLES: I thought, this year, I *decided* the lecture series would be organized around the theme of American extremism in various forms: political, religious, etcetera. And that it was time—high time, if you ask me—for a monster such as Carver to be exposed—debated and exposed—for the evil, hateful cretin that he is.

QUINN: I see. Are you writing something about Carver, about their movement?

CHARLES: No, I'm—no.

QUINN: Ah. Well, you can—I'm sure you can understand my asking.

CHARLES: Yes, no, of course.

QUINN: That it *would* be in your wheelhouse, if you—

CHARLES: Absolutely. A fair question.

QUINN: Mm.

CHARLES: As, as you know, I've already written a book about people who *join* movements like this. Right now I'm more interested in the people who *leave*. Who disavow, subvert, resist. *That's* the book I'm writing.

QUINN: Sounds like my kind of book. So, what's it about?

(During the following, CHARLES stands. Despite his current state, he awakens when talking about this. Something comes alive in him, the instructor, the lecture hall orator. We see a glimpse of the brilliance and dynamism that made the man the legend.)

CHARLES: Spring, 1941. Late one night in the dark skies over Britain, a lone German Messerschmitt plane cleaved its way through dense fog. When the aircraft

ran out of fuel, it crashed in a farmer's field near
Glasgow. The pilot, who had parachuted to safety, was
a high-ranking Nazi named Rudolf Hess. When he was
found, Hess demanded to see members of the British
Parliament, with whom he thought he could realize his
wild dream of brokering a peace behind Churchill's
back.

QUINN: Right. But Hess didn't "leave the movement"
so much as get locked up and spend the rest of the war
in British prisons.

CHARLES: Precisely, very good. Which is why my book
is not *about* Hess—not entirely. Because—*because*—
there is an unknown history. Hess had an advisor
named Albrecht Haushofer. *(Gaining steam)* Now. I've
been digging through primary sources of the era. Rare,
scattered official records, interviews conducted by
the Allies after the German surrender…and I may be
closing in on some very interesting material related to
Haushofer.

AMY: I'm sorry, but is this really the time to—

QUINN: I'm interested.

CHARLES: *(Excitement evident)* Thank you. So.
Haushofer was no run-of-the-mill Nazi. Having
a half-Jewish mother meant he had quarter-grade
Jewish blood. Inevitably a death sentence. But because
Hess was a close friend of the family, he saw to it
that Haushofer was issued a proper German blood
certificate. Haushofer was a professor of some renown,
with a perch of relative safety, but as the years ground
on, he grew…disillusioned. Germany was fracturing.
Call it a moral collapse. The spaces he inhabited, the
company he kept…there, it was impossible to ignore
the growing chorus of angry, terrified whispers…
the rumors of camps, atrocities. He decided that
something had to be done. So, he risked his life to

join the resistance. Now, it's, it's always been known
that Haushofer was involved somehow in Hess'
brazen flight, but no one could prove the extent of
it—or exactly what transpired. *(Pause)* But earlier
this year I heard a rumor. From one of my sources in
Munich—a *friend*, really—we first met years ago when
I was researching the book you read. The rumor is
that Haushofer kept a diary. A diary of those months
leading up to and following the spring of 1941.
Haushofer's diary—in his own words! To see it there,
in my own hands…the ink on the page…the entire
history of the affair told by the man who, in secret,
played the strongest role in guiding it. Just astonishing.

QUINN: "My own hands"?

CHARLES: Hm?

QUINN: "In my own hands." You said—

CHARLES: I'm sorry, I don't follow.

QUINN: You said, "To see it there, in my own hands…"
(Pause) So, you've seen it?

CHARLES: Seen…?

QUINN: The diary.

(Beat)

CHARLES: No, I…what did I say? I said—

QUINN: Did someone show you this diary?

(A long, painful beat)

AMY: Charles?

(Another beat)

QUINN: Mr Nichols. If there is something else to know,
we will come to know it. And it is infinitely better
for you…if you tell me about it yourself. Do you
understand?

(CHARLES, *suppressing fear, nods.*)

QUINN: I'll ask again. Did someone show you this diary?

(CHARLES *studies* QUINN. *Then he looks to* AMY.)

(*Cornered, he makes a decision.*)

(CHARLES, *pained, turns back to* QUINN.)

CHARLES: Yes.

QUINN: Who?

CHARLES: Carver sent a man.

AMY: Dammit, Charles, no…

QUINN: The man's name?

CHARLES: I wasn't told. And look—I, I want to be clear. It was always the plan to expose Carver.

QUINN: (*Consults notes*) So, Mr Carver has the… Haushofer diary.

CHARLES: Yes. He…through one of his contacts in Switzerland, a private collector aligned with his, with the *movement*…Carver came into possession of it. Soon after, he reached out to me.

QUINN: Because of your lecture series. Which is prestigious.

AMY: The most prestigious.

CHARLES: For him to speak here…would be of great value. And for me, a period source like the Haushofer diary is of great value. It's enough to build a book on.

QUINN: So, you worked out a deal. Would you describe it as a trade?

CHARLES: Yes. The diary for the speech. (*To* AMY) I'm sorry. I'm so sorry.

(*Beat*)

QUINN: The trip to Maine. Was it to get the diary?

CHARLES: No. He said he wanted to feel me out. See if he could trust me. He was showing off.

(QUINN *makes notes.*)

QUINN: When were you to receive the diary?

CHARLES: After the lecture, his lecture.

QUINN: Does Lucas Poole know about this arrangement?

CHARLES: No. No one does.

AMY: How would you find it? (*Pause*) The diary. Because of your connection to Carver…people might wonder if he had a hand in it. You couldn't have that.

CHARLES: (*Ashamed*) Next summer. I have a research trip to Munich planned. After traveling with it, I would…find it in some archive there.

(AMY *takes a breath and hangs her head.*)

(*Beat*)

(QUINN *closes the notebook.*)

CHARLES: You know…I mean you *understand* where I was coming from. What I was aiming to do to this, this horrible man. There's no—just no way I could have foreseen what happened.

QUINN: (*Pause*) I work for a federal agency that is predominantly male, overwhelmingly White, and to say it "leans conservative" is something of an understatement. So, I've seen and heard it all. Now…I *did* assume that Boston—even good old *Boston*—would be an improvement over the part of Tennessee where I grew up. But from time to time, we're all guilty of a little wishful thinking.

CHARLES: What—what is happening…?

QUINN: I wasn't supposed to be here. One of my colleagues was assigned to your interview. Murphy.

You would have liked him. But I asked my supervisor if I could step in. I wanted to be the one to sit across from you. I knew that the man who wrote that book would not invite Carver to speak. There had to be something else. And I will say. Having my gut instinct confirmed is normally a rush. But this time? Very disappointing. *(She stands to gather her things.)* I think that's all for the moment. The Bureau will be in touch as things move ahead. *(Pause)* A word of advice. You should retain counsel.

CHARLES: But I—for what?

QUINN: Not for us. Assuming what you've told me is true—

CHARLES: It is true, and there's nothing more.

QUINN: Assuming that, it's unlikely you'll find yourself in criminal jeopardy. But the possibility of a civil case. The university *has* lawyers.

CHARLES: Wait. Wait. You think the family will sue?

QUINN: If, somehow, you found yourself in their position…wouldn't you? *(Pause)* Thank you, Mr Nichols. Oh—your notes.

(QUINN indicates CHARLES' legal pad. He picks it up and tears off the pages he wrote on. Then hands them over.)

(After a last look at CHARLES, QUINN exits.)

(Beat)

(CHARLES looks at AMY. It takes a few moments before she can look up at him. She is simmering with anger.)

AMY: While you may not have been able to foresee this, you should have feared it. But you carried on without a thought for anyone but yourself, saying "This is about free speech", obviously a lie in retrospect, which is clarifying, so thank you.

CHARLES: That was *not* a lie—

AMY: (*Over him*) You went ahead—

CHARLES: Amy—

AMY: (*Over him*) No—you went, went ahead with this for a *book*? Just help me understand that. Why?

CHARLES: Oh, God, Amy…

AMY: Why?

CHARLES: Because I, I felt like…I feel like I'm on my way out.

AMY: What are you talking about? You're a tenured professor.

CHARLES: Not out of the university…out of the game.

AMY: You should have come to me. You should have been honest with me.

CHARLES: Okay. Okay. This is bad—I see that, I see that, I do—but here's something that can make it, at least *start* to make it less so, to, to smooth things over. Here…

(CHARLES *grabs a folder from his desk.*)

CHARLES: My statement, here, we put *this* out…
and, *and*, Maggie had organized a meeting, a "safe" meeting, a sit-down with Hillel and the, ah, the Black Students Association—let's do that—to talk to students. We can convene, and talk, an open dialogue about all of this, to—

AMY: No.

CHARLES: Please, it would be good—we, everyone can talk about it—

AMY: No one wants that.

(AMY *and* CHARLES *lock eyes. Her clear disappointment in him is overwhelming to them both.*)

AMY: You're being put on administrative leave.

CHARLES: Now, hang on, just, just—

AMY: Deliberations on your dismissal begin next week.

CHARLES: Wait, come on…

AMY: No contact with students. Your ID swipe has already been disabled.

CHARLES: Amy, just—slow down—

AMY: I'll need your keys. And while you're on leave, you can't come back to campus.

CHARLES: STOP. JUST STOP. Hang on—okay? Hang on. And you're—the agent just walked out of my fucking office and already—

AMY: It was decided this morning. First thing.

CHARLES: You can't do this. I didn't kill her.

AMY: Nobody's saying you killed her—

CHARLES: Thank you! So, yes, so together, we simply—

AMY: It's done. The press release is going out.

CHARLES: But…but please…why are you not protecting me? This is *me*…

AMY: In this climate. What you've done. A young woman is dead. One of our students.

CHARLES: I know that.

AMY: Charles. A young, Black woman. Murdered by a White nationalist.

CHARLES: I know that. I know that.

AMY: And this is before we even knew about the diary, this trade. I don't know how it could look worse.

CHARLES: "How it could look." Uh-huh. Uh-huh. Well. A lot of things could look pretty bad.

AMY: You're not making sense.

CHARLES: I suppose you, what, you think I'd go quietly.

AMY: What does that mean?

CHARLES: Cut the shit.

AMY: What does it mean?

CHARLES: What we've discussed? Back and forth?

AMY: What are you talking about?

CHARLES: There are records. Of written things. That's how e-mail works. I bet people would love to get their eyes on those.

AMY: I don't know what e-mails you're talking about.

CHARLES: What are you—are you kidding me? You have memory loss? (*He goes around the desk to his computer. He types, scrolls, and reads. But it's clear he's not finding what he's looking for. He stops, incredulous, then looks at her.*) What the fuck is this? Where are they?

AMY: Where are what?

CHARLES: Goddammit, you *know* what.

AMY: I honestly have no idea what you're talking about.

CHARLES: This is…no. No way. Fuck this. This is—

AMY: Charles—

CHARLES: NOT A CHANCE. I will not go. I've been— my *family's* been a part of this university for five generations. FIVE. Students, deans, professors. Their souls are in these walls. And now—what—it's over? I'm supposed to *accept* that? And the president won't even speak to me?

AMY: He'll speak to you. I just wanted to speak to you first. I'm your friend.

CHARLES: You're not my friend. My what? You're not my fucking friend. You've pulled, I don't even know, some kind of—

(*CRASH! A brick careens through the window. It flies across the room, hits the glass case containing the model sailboat. Everything shatters. It's a splintered mess of glass shards and broken wood.*)

(CHARLES *is frozen, looking at the wreckage.* AMY *darts to the window, looks out.*)

AMY: Shit. (*Calls security from* CHARLES' *desk phone; into phone*) This is Dean Katz, let me speak to Sergeant D'Avella. (*Waits*) Tony, hi. I'm in Robinson Hall 204, just had a brick thrown through the window… Charles Nichols… No, they were gone. And no one's hurt… Thanks. (*She hangs up the phone.*)

(CHARLES *pulls the brick from the pile of debris. A piece of paper is rubber-banded to the brick.*)

(CHARLES *removes the paper, unfolds it, and reads what is block-printed on it.*)

CHARLES: "Fuck you Nazi." (*He drops the paper. He kneels to pick out the pieces of his boat model from the glass.*)

AMY: You'll cut yourself.

(*Ignoring her,* CHARLES *continues.*)

AMY: Don't. Charles. Charles. Charlie.

(CHARLES *doesn't stop.* AMY *watches him.*)

(*Lights down*)

Scene Four

(Lights up on a home office. Enough full bookshelves to be a lending library. One shelf displays a small but carefully curated collection of Judaica. It's no more than four or five items, of which one is an aged, heirloom Hanukkiah.)

(MAGGIE is seated with a bag at her feet. She holds an iPad. She's nervous. She fidgets.)

(AMY enters with two glasses of water.)

AMY: No ice.

MAGGIE: Thank you.

AMY: Eliot is asleep upstairs, so we should try to keep it down.

MAGGIE: Of course. How is he?

AMY: *(Inscrutable; guard up)* Hanging in. You said there was something urgent.

MAGGIE: Yes.

AMY: You seem nervous.

MAGGIE: I am.

AMY: *(Pause; with care)* Have you been hurt?

MAGGIE: No.

AMY: Good.

MAGGIE: No, it's… *(Her breath quickens. She calms herself down.)* Thank you for welcoming me into your home. I'd like your help with something.

AMY: Okay…

MAGGIE: You know Professor Nichols has gone to meet him. Carver.

AMY: Charles made me aware.

MAGGIE: I, ah. I got a text from one of my students. They're up there. In Maine.

AMY: The *students* are in Maine?

MAGGIE: To protest. Yes. She said they're at the compound now.

AMY: But Charles didn't even know the address. How did they—

MAGGIE: You'd have to ask them.

(MAGGIE *is stalling.* AMY *can tell.*)

AMY: You said you'd like my help.

MAGGIE: Yes. Yes. And first I should just say, I was as surprised as I'm sure you're going to be. Because I respect him.

AMY: "Him."

MAGGIE: But it appears that—Professor Nichols. That he has not been entirely forthright about his dealings with Carver.

AMY: No?

MAGGIE: No. And when I think about them, up there right now, sharing a meal together…

AMY: *(Moving on)* In what way. Has Professor Nichols been less than forthright.

MAGGIE: In kind of a bad one. And I think something should be done about it.

(Beat)

AMY: Two years ago you took my seminar.

MAGGIE: *(With admiration)* You changed the way I thought about it all—gender and power and, and resistance. It was important to me. So important.

AMY: I remember it was. So, as a favor to me now: get to the point.

MAGGIE: *(Pause)* There's a diary. A period source. Some Nazi advisor. Carver has it and he's giving it to Nichols.

AMY: "Giving it to him."

MAGGIE: Trading it, actually. For the speaking engagement here. An exchange.

(AMY*'s blood boils. She remains calm.*)

AMY: Assuming this is true, how did you find it out?

MAGGIE: I accessed the professor's e-mails.

AMY: That's a crime.

MAGGIE: Especially how I did it.

(MAGGIE *hands over the iPad.* AMY *reads. Scrolls down. As she reads more, her anger and concern grow steadily.*)

MAGGIE: He told us about the Carver invitation last week. Lucas and me, Charles told us. Not about the diary and the trade, of course. So, I tried to talk Charles out of it, you know, gently, but I'm sick of that. I hate the way I've had to talk to him. Hat-in-hand, and aw-shucks, and if I raise my voice even a little, he just totally disengages. So, last night, when the list came out, finally I could do something. I sat with the undergrads helping them organize, strategize. But this is *Charles*, so…we both know a meeting with students was a long-shot at best. I had to do more. *(Loaded)* I remember reading a book about that when I was in high school…about women having to do their resistance work in the shadows. Feel like it won some kind of prize.

(AMY *looks up from the iPad.* AMY *and* MAGGIE *hold eye contact.*)

(Then AMY *hands the iPad back. As* MAGGIE *takes it, it's clear her fortitude has grown. She is hitting a stride.*)

AMY: Maggie, I want you to listen to me very carefully—

MAGGIE: This is wrong. You know it's wrong. You can end it.

AMY: What's wrong—and I'm having trouble keeping straight the multiple inappropriate moves you've made here tonight—

MAGGIE: "*I've* made."

AMY: What's wrong is that you've broken the law—

MAGGIE: These are *Nazis*. That *I've* broken the law?

AMY: Disciplinary action will be taken—

MAGGIE: Why are you protecting him? It isn't what you *write* about, what you *teach*—

AMY: I suggest you go now.

MAGGIE: But I haven't told you what I want yet.

AMY: Good night, Maggie.

MAGGIE: As a Jew you're a fucking disgrace.

AMY: Excuse me?

MAGGIE: You know where this is heading. I thought we stood against that.

(*Off the look in* AMY's *eyes*)

MAGGIE: There—that's right. I can see you agree. So why don't you do something? Why isn't anyone doing anything? He's up there having dinner with these people right now! I feel like I'm on crazy pills. Who am *I*? I have no power. I'm a Ph.D. candidate with sixty grand in loan debt. You have a *voice*—a voice you should be using, standing on a rooftop, shredding your vocal cords to keep Nazis and the Ku Klux fucking Klan off your campus.

AMY: Try to imagine being part of the team that runs a university like this one.

MAGGIE: You don't feel an obligation, a moral obligation, to stand up, no matter what it costs?

AMY: I don't know how to answer that.

MAGGIE: I think you just did.

AMY: I am stunned that you think you can come in here and talk to me this way.

MAGGIE: It's safe to assume that after the e-mail thing, I don't have much else to lose.

AMY: This means that much to you.

MAGGIE: Yes! Frankly I'm astonished that it *doesn't* to you.

AMY: You have no idea what it means to me.

MAGGIE: I *thought* I did. I *thought* I knew you. I know your home because I've been your guest here. I know your story because you've told it to me. *(Points to bookshelf)* I know that's your great-grandmother's Hanukkiah. That she lugged across the Pale while she was pregnant with your grandfather, running from the secret police. One suitcase—just the one, right? Gotta travel light when you're fleeing Minsk at nineteen, knocked-up—oh and you're *alone* because your husband, along with dozens of other men, was shot in a ditch.

AMY: Don't talk about them.

MAGGIE: I think I *will*. I think I *need* to. I think you, and I'm sorry, I am, but *you* need to consider how they'd feel about this bullshit, kid-gloved, let's-have-a-civil-debate nonsense. Is that what you do with Cossacks? With Nazis? With the Klan? Your family, our families…you're failing them. By doing nothing.

AMY: We have procedures here.

MAGGIE: *Yeah*, you do.

AMY: What does that mean?

MAGGIE: This is what it means. This is what you're going to do: you will contact Carver and tell him he is not welcome on this campus. Either at Nichols' symposium, or any other student-run, non-university-sanctioned event. That his footsteps on this campus will be considered an act of trespassing and police will be called.

AMY: I can't do that. This is America.

MAGGIE: For now. And you can do it. You will.

AMY: "I will." And why's that?

MAGGIE: Because of the other e-mails. Between the two of you, you and Professor Nichols. You mentioned the law. Well. Title IX is a law. But two years ago…when Nichols wrote to you about one of his female students who was distraught, who couldn't recall the details of a drunken sexual encounter with a classmate… you told him to encourage the student to keep quiet, not report it…because the other student, the probable date-rapist, is from a family with its name on a campus building. *(Beat)* Or last month…when Nichols caught an undergraduate plagiarizing, he e-mailed you before confronting the student. To ask for your guidance. Because the student's mother is some big Hollywood producer. And you told him… *(Taps iPad screen; reads)* "I think we can let this one go."

AMY: You've made your point.

MAGGIE: That it would *look* bad, is my point. If that got out. Imagine if that little tidbit found its way to the great journalistic minds at Breitbart. The headline. "Coastal, liberal elites protect unethical son of Hollywood globalist."

AMY: Enough.

MAGGIE: And "globalist" means "Jew". You know that, right? *(Pause)* If you cared about protecting this university from Nazis as much as you care about protecting its donors—

(AMY quickly steps close to MAGGIE, speaks sharply.)

AMY: I leaked. The list. Of speakers. *(A long beat)* Since we're baring all. You can't really think I want him to come here.

(MAGGIE reacts, seeing AMY in a new light.)

AMY: You have no clue—absolutely NONE—what I've been doing. What a great number of us have been doing without your knowledge, or anyone's. Because why *should* you know? *(Pause)* We all have our ways of trying. This, apparently, is yours. *(She goes to the desk and sits down at her laptop.)* What is Carver's e-mail address?

(MAGGIE, processing, stands still.)

AMY: Well, do you want me to ruin their dinner, or not?

(MAGGIE hands over the iPad. AMY copies down the e-mail address, then types. MAGGIE watches her.)

AMY: *(Without looking up)* Hacking the e-mails. I'm assuming you had help. No offense.

MAGGIE: None taken. Yes. I had a contact.

AMY: I don't know a lot about computers. But this contact. Clearly they can dig things up.

MAGGIE: Yes.

AMY: Can they make things disappear?

(AMY does not look up from her screen. MAGGIE looks at her. Lights fade, leaving only the laptop glow on AMY.)

Scene Two

(Lights come up on a downmarket bar.)

(LUCAS is seated at a table. He's on his phone, scrolling, reading. There is a bottle of beer on the table.)

(BAXTER enters. He notices LUCAS and approaches.)

BAXTER: Hey!

(LUCAS looks up, sees BAXTER.)

LUCAS: Hello.

BAXTER: Quick drink before the trip.

LUCAS: Yeah.

BAXTER: Charles mentioned he's meeting you here.

LUCAS: He texted, said he's running late.

BAXTER: Yup. I was on the phone with him, he said he had to run home, pick something up. So, we've got some time. Do I order at the bar, or does he come over?

LUCAS: Oh, you want a drink?

BAXTER: *(Laughs)* I think I'll have one, yeah.

LUCAS: It's pretty dead in here, Frank's probably swapping out the kegs. *(Calls out)* Hey, ah, Frank…? *(To BAXTER)* Or he's restocking the pretzels. If you're hungry, you can ask for a bowl—but they are consistently, phenomenally stale.

(FRANK enters. Towel over his shoulder. Apron around his waist. The Platonic ideal of a bartender.)

FRANK: Afternoon!

BAXTER: Hi, how you doing?

FRANK: Good, what're you havin?

BAXTER: Basil Hayden's neat and a Sam Adams.

FRANK: Okay.

LUCAS: Frank, this is Baxter Forrest. He's famous.

BAXTER: Not really.

FRANK: Wow.

LUCAS: He's on television.

FRANK: I never seen ya.

LUCAS: He's a famous professor.

BAXTER: Come on, now.

(*An awkward beat*)

FRANK: That's great. Basil neat, Sam back. (*He exits off to the bar.*)

BAXTER: Charles speaks highly of you.

LUCAS: I appreciate him doing that.

BAXTER: (*Pause*) So. Where are *you* on this?

LUCAS: "On"…

BAXTER: Carver coming to speak.

LUCAS: It would…certainly avoid a lot of trouble if he didn't.

BAXTER: Well, that's the idea. Which is why I figured… swing by here…me and another voice that Charles respects…maybe we can talk some sense into him.

LUCAS: Oh. I, ah…think his mind is pretty much made up?

BAXTER: 'Til it isn't. Can't hurt to try, right?

(*Beat*)

(LUCAS *takes a sip of his beer.*)

BAXTER: He tells me you applied for the fellowship.

LUCAS: I did.

BAXTER: Mm. What's your focus?

LUCAS: Seventeenth-century Sweden.

BAXTER: Okay. Cool.

LUCAS: Sort of *have* to apply…

BAXTER: For the fellowship, sure. It's one of the top—

LUCAS: If not *the* top.

BAXTER: Correct.

LUCAS: *You* had it.

BAXTER: I did.

LUCAS: Was it easy for you to get?

BAXTER: No. Why would it be easy?

LUCAS: I don't know. But you got it.

BAXTER: If you get it…will it have been easy for you?

LUCAS: Definitely not.

BAXTER: There you go.

LUCAS: But you did get it.

BAXTER: And you might.

LUCAS: "I might."

BAXTER: You might have it. The fellowship.

LUCAS: *(Pause)* Oh.

BAXTER: Charles likes you. I'm just saying.

LUCAS: Well, we have to apply a lot of places.

BAXTER: Sure. But, you know, another way to think about it. In terms of getting Charles to see this clearly and make the right call. Is if *he* takes a serious hit on this, as far as reputation, the fellowship might not stick around. One of the best jobs in our field. Gone. Is that ideal…?

(Beat)

LUCAS: I'm gonna let you in on a little secret. This is not my first drink.

BAXTER: Okay.

LUCAS: I'm celebrating.

BAXTER: You are, huh.

LUCAS: I got the call this morning. In Charles' office, you were standing right there. I got an offer.

BAXTER: Hey, good for you.

LUCAS: Right. Yeah. Thank you.

BAXTER: Do you mind me asking where?

LUCAS: I'd rather not say for now.

BAXTER: I get it. Cheers. What do they say in Sweden?

LUCAS: Skål.

BAXTER: Skål.

(LUCAS *laughs.* BAXTER *wonders why, but doesn't ask.*)

BAXTER: It's a good offer?

LUCAS: Assistant professor, tenure track.

BAXTER: Wow. Nice, that's—I'm impressed. Your work must be strong. I mean, you're—how old are you?

LUCAS: Twenty-nine.

BAXTER: Yeah, so. Nicely done. Must be strong in lectures, too.

LUCAS: I did debate in high school. I like speaking in front of crowds.

BAXTER: Are you thinking—I mean, if you do get the fellowship—are you thinking of not accepting?

LUCAS: Not accepting the fellowship?

BAXTER: No—not accepting the other job. I don't know. Is it a top school?

LUCAS: We might define "top school" differently.

BAXTER: Hey, I'm just asking.

LUCAS: I would consider not accepting the fellowship. You seem surprised.

BAXTER: Not necessarily.

LUCAS: You *would* be surprised.

(FRANK *comes over with* BAXTER's *round. He sets the glasses on the table, blind to the tension between the men.*)

FRANK: Basil neat, Sam back. Hey, you two want to hear a joke?

LUCAS: We're okay.

FRANK: It's about a pirate.

BAXTER: We're good, sir. Thank you.

(FRANK, *a little deflated, walks off.*)

BAXTER: Do you have a problem with me?

LUCAS: Your assumption—that I would pass up a job, a real job, because it's not on one of the coasts, or in *Chicago*—

BAXTER: I don't know where the job is. And I don't make assumptions, brother.

LUCAS: You absolutely do, you said—

BAXTER: I *didn't* say—

LUCAS: You *did*. You said—

BAXTER: I *asked*—if you would take the job over the fellowship. A question.

LUCAS: Your *tone*. The *way* you asked, this assumption. It's perfect, actually.

BAXTER: Hey—I don't give a shit what you do.

LUCAS: It's Iowa State.

BAXTER: *(Pause)* That's a great school.

LUCAS: "Great school."

BAXTER: Jesus, man. Now what.

LUCAS: Your tone. Your whole…POV…is so coastal. So elite.

BAXTER: "Coastal." "Elite." Like your Harvard doctoral program.

LUCAS: You're on their team. I'm not.

BAXTER: You're not?

LUCAS: White male. "Cis-het." Straight White male.

BAXTER: Oh. Oh. Okay.

LUCAS: Tell me. Go ahead. Tell me one thing it's worse to be right now.

(Beat)

BAXTER: This is interesting.

LUCAS: Yeah.

BAXTER: Never met one in the wild before. Normally just up in my mentions. Blank avatar. The face of bravery.

LUCAS: I read your book. It's a real piece of shit.

BAXTER: If it offended you, which it seems to have, that's a compliment.

LUCAS: You write about code-switching like Blacks are the only ones who do it. Who choose to.

BAXTER: I didn't frame it like that.

LUCAS: Well, you didn't frame *anything* in the book, but that's a separate issue.

(Beat)

(BAXTER *takes a sip of his beer.*)

BAXTER: Fuck it. I can't wait to hear you. Tell me. About code-switching.

LUCAS: Act and talk one way here, another over here. Different roles for different crowds. Blending in.

Keeping secrets. *Surviving.* You think you're the only ones who do that? I'm switching codes every day. I'm a fuckin switchboard operator.

BAXTER: What are your codes?

LUCAS: Where I'm from? What my parents do? I've been in hiding with these people for years. These schools are fuckin synagogues.

BAXTER: It's subtle, but I'm picking up definite signals of…economic anxiety. *(Pause)* Not a chance Charles knows this about you.

LUCAS: Of course not. I'm only being honest with you because I'm in a good mood.

BAXTER: Wonder what he'd say if he found out.

LUCAS: You could tell him. But I'm his golden boy. You're an old student with a career that drives him insane with jealousy. Safe money's on my word against yours.

BAXTER: You think Iowa State will be as easy to convince?

LUCAS: I'm not afraid of you. You want to "out" me? There's nothing to *out.* I have never so much as liked the wrong tweet. There are no questionable blog posts under a pen name. It wouldn't be worth it for a big, famous scholar like you to punch down…and miss.

BAXTER: Mm. Well, I gotta own this one. Went looking for a wingman, but reached out to the wrong Caucasian. Hate it when that happens.

LUCAS: It's telling—it says a lot, it does—that you don't think Carver should be allowed to speak.

BAXTER: *Here.* I don't think he should be allowed to speak *here.* Plenty of places he's free to: public park, podcast, warming up the crowd for Ted Cruz at a gun show.

LUCAS: Typical, that's—see? That's such a typical lib move, stereotyping conservatives while being outright *hostile* to the very concept of free speech.

BAXTER: This isn't about free speech—and do not patronize me by acting like you don't know that—but I will grant you, it's been a clever way to get what you *actually* want.

LUCAS: Which is?

BAXTER: You're not original, by the way. Part of some vanguard. You probably feel transgressive—brave, even. But you are singing an old song. This song is old as hell.

LUCAS: What is it. That you think I want.

BAXTER: You want…to launder eliminationist, genocidal politics through the sanitizing spin cycle of speaking engagements and panel discussions at colleges and universities like this one.

LUCAS: *You* said "genocide", not me.

BAXTER: That *is* what the hoods and the swastikas mean.

LUCAS: Oh, relax. You're too focused on a few outlier symbols. And since when're people not allowed to ask the hard questions?

BAXTER: *Six*-year-olds ask the hard questions. "Where does the universe end?" *That's* a hard question. You're questioning, what…"White genocide"? That's not a thing. Your persecution is imagined. But you people know what you're doing.

LUCAS: "You people." Interesting…

BAXTER: I saw the gaming headset on your bag this morning. So, what was it—some Nazis find you on a Discord channel while you were playing Call of Duty? They nurse your little grievances? Recruit you to the cause? Laugh when you pronounced it with a hard "R"?

LUCAS: You really believe what comes out of the mainstream media.

BAXTER: My guy, I'm *in* the mainstream media.

LUCAS: That's your problem! You're like a child, swimming with those, those...inflatable things on his arms. Obviously afraid to get in the deep water and have a real debate.

BAXTER: First of all, I get paid to debate. I get paid to *talk*. You're getting this one for free, which—you know, against my better judgement. Normally I don't mud-wrestle with pigs.

LUCAS: Oh, that's, that's—

BAXTER: *(Over him)* I get what you're going for, though, I see it...the path you're charting. Iowa State. You're off to the "heartland". Bigger student body. Set up shop, get tenure, write some books.

LUCAS: Run for Congress.

BAXTER: Well. You'll have plenty of friends when you get there.

LUCAS: Not nearly enough. But there will be soon.

BAXTER: Guess we'll see.

(In the stillness, BAXTER *and* LUCAS *study each other.)*

LUCAS: We met before. At the Columbia conference last year. You don't remember me?

BAXTER: No.

LUCAS: Mm. Can I toss out a theory? I think you're the one who's worried. If your old mentor goes up in flames over this, will that effect your speaking fees? Your next book advance?

*(*BAXTER *remains stoic, but* LUCAS *sees that he hit a nerve.)*

LUCAS: You've barely touched your drinks.

BAXTER: Want to stay sharp.

LUCAS: I'll bet. Did it ever occur to you that I know Charles a lot better than you do?

BAXTER: Hadn't thought about it.

LUCAS: Because I can tell—not that he's come right out and said it—but I can sense these things. We usually can. People like Charles…the "free speech" thing is their cover. And if it's *not* their cover—then it's *our way in.*

BAXTER: Oh, I see plenty of that. Shit, a *lifetime* of that. But Charlie isn't like you.

LUCAS: No? Let's run a test. I'm about to get on a train with him. I'll see what I can coax out. Baseline, entry-level stuff. See if I can get him to agree in the abstract that "White pride" is a valid thing. Use the right rhetorical strategies…you'd be surprised what White people will reveal about their secret hearts.

BAXTER: Nothing about White people surprises me. And you're reading too many message boards. Twitter is not the real world.

LUCAS: I knew it was only a matter of time before you lectured me about "realness", brother.

BAXTER: You're a sad, small man who's fooled a lot of good people.

LUCAS: Well, game recognize game, right? As the rappers say? You have fooled the entire liberal-media industrial complex into thinking you're smarter than you are. You're not advanced—you're just articulate.

BAXTER: Here it comes.

LUCAS: You have a ceiling on you. So enjoy your fifteen minutes. But Lord knows those minutes are a test for the rest of us. To have to watch you, sitting on the television, flapping those lips.

(*A long beat*)

BAXTER: It will not work. You won't get the rise you want from me.

LUCAS: I don't want a fuckin thing from you.

BAXTER: Okay.

LUCAS: It doesn't matter, you know. How many books you publish. How many times you're on TV. End of the day, when push comes to shove—and it will—it's always going to be my country, not yours.

BAXTER: (*Smiles*) Knew we'd eventually agree on something. (*He stands, drops money on the table, enough to cover all the drinks. Loaded:*) By the way, I've got a friend in the history department at Iowa State. You probably met her at the Columbia conference. I'll text her, put in a word.

(FRANK *enters with a bowl of pretzels.*)

FRANK: You fellas need anything?

BAXTER: I'm heading out…but you know what, my good man? (*Hands money to* FRANK; *nods to* LUCAS) Let's have another round for this guy. Jägermeister. (*He walks out.*)

(LUCAS *sits stewing.*)

FRANK: You want a shot'a Jäger?

LUCAS: No.

(LUCAS, *rattled, takes* BAXTER's *whiskey and downs it in one.* FRANK *shrugs, pockets the bill* BAXTER *handed him.*)

FRANK: You gonna have his beer, too?

LUCAS: No, he drank from that.

(FRANK *picks up* BAXTER's *beer.* LUCAS *eats stale pretzels.*)

FRANK: How 'bout that joke now?

(LUCAS *looks offstage, sees something.*)

LUCAS: Maybe in a little bit—my friend is here.

(MAGGIE *enters. She approaches the table.*)

FRANK: Not a problem. This'll build up anticipation. (*To* MAGGIE) Hey, what can I get ya?

MAGGIE: Nothing, but thank you.

(FRANK *heads off to the bar.*)

LUCAS: Hi.

MAGGIE: This place is a dump.

LUCAS: It's not.

MAGGIE: Was that—I was crossing the street—was Baxter Forrest in here?

LUCAS: Yeah.

MAGGIE: Did you talk to him?

LUCAS: (*Sharp; agitated*) Not really. So, what was so urgent?

MAGGIE: Whoa. Are you…is everything okay?

LUCAS: (*Covering*) Yeah. Yeah yeah, sorry. What's up, why did you want to meet?

MAGGIE: (*Nervous*) Oh. Ah…well… (*Pause*) Do you think Dean Katz will find out who leaked the list of speakers?

LUCAS: It's not like she runs a crack team of investigators. She glad-hands alumni.

MAGGIE: She's literally the best professor I've ever studied with.

LUCAS: Right, the biennial feminism seminar. I missed that one.

MAGGIE: Such a prick.

LUCAS: C'mon. *You* texted *me*. And Charles'll be here any minute.

MAGGIE: I don't know how to, ah…even broach this…

LUCAS: Okay.

MAGGIE: Can I…can this be private?

LUCAS: Of course.

MAGGIE: I need your help. I want to ask for your help with something. Your message boards and, whatever, chat rooms…

LUCAS: "Whatever chat rooms."

MAGGIE: You know, I don't know what—where you post, and—with your video game friends.

LUCAS: Okay.

MAGGIE: You know people, or you talk to them, who are good with computers.

LUCAS: Yeah.

MAGGIE: And you are, you're good with computers.

LUCAS: Not as good as some of these guys.

MAGGIE: Well, I'm hoping—can you introduce me to one of them?

LUCAS: Why?

MAGGIE: Honestly? I don't want to say too much. But. To access something.

LUCAS: Access what.

MAGGIE: E-mail. Someone's account.

LUCAS: *(Pause)* Huh.

MAGGIE: Yeah.

LUCAS: Would not have guessed.

MAGGIE: Well.

LUCAS: I don't even want to know what this is about.

MAGGIE: That's good.

LUCAS: It's a crime. You'd be doing crime.

MAGGIE: I'm aware. But you do know people.

(LUCAS *studies* MAGGIE. *Then decides.*)

LUCAS: I might know one guy.

MAGGIE: Okay.

LUCAS: You'll have to pay.

MAGGIE: How much?

LUCAS: Just e-mail?

(MAGGIE *nods "yes".*)

LUCAS: Not much. Do you know what Bitcoin is?

MAGGIE: No one knows what Bitcoin is.

LUCAS: In a pinch I bet he'll take Venmo. (*He takes out his phone, begins typing on the screen.*)

MAGGIE: What are you doing?

(LUCAS *keeps typing on the phone.*)

MAGGIE: Are you writing to him?

LUCAS: (*Still typing*) Take out your phone.

(MAGGIE *takes out her phone.* LUCAS *lays his phone on the table, its screen facing* MAGGIE.)

LUCAS: Copy that down. All of that.

MAGGIE: What is it?

LUCAS: Someone like this, you don't write to their Gmail address. You have to download a separate browser—

MAGGIE: I can't use Safari?

LUCAS: (*Pause*) No. You have to download something called Tor.

MAGGIE: "Tor."

LUCAS: Just—just copy that down. It's a message board. And a username to contact. You'll create a username of your own. Not your real name.

MAGGIE: I'm tech-illiterate, not a fucking imbecile.

LUCAS: Whatever you're doing, don't get caught.

MAGGIE: I won't. *(She slides his phone back across the table.)*

*(*LUCAS *deletes what he wrote on his phone.)*

LUCAS: So you know. I will deny we ever spoke.

MAGGIE: We didn't speak.

LUCAS: That's good. One drink. Stay for one.

MAGGIE: I'm leaving.

LUCAS: One drink.

MAGGIE: You're a fuckin alcoholic.

LUCAS: At least I know what Bitcoin is.

*(*CHARLES *enters the bar, sees them, and approaches.)*

CHARLES: Hello!

LUCAS: *(To* MAGGIE*; quiet)* What, no "thank you"?

MAGGIE: *(Quiet)* Thank you.

*(*CHARLES *signals offstage to Frank to order a drink.* MAGGIE *stands. She pulls a book from her bag.)*

MAGGIE: Hi, Charles.

CHARLES: Did Lucas change your mind about the trip?

MAGGIE: No, I—

LUCAS: Try as I might... *(To* MAGGIE*)* There's always plenty of room on these trains.

MAGGIE: (*To* CHARLES) I just came to get—Lucas had a book of mine. (*Holds up the book*) I'm teaching this on Thursday. So…

CHARLES: Ah.

MAGGIE: Got home, realized—then had to come all the way out here.

CHARLES: Well, you saved me a phone call. Wanted to say I'm sorry.

MAGGIE: For…?

CHARLES: I pushed a little hard in my office earlier. About you coming with. Of *course* this is different for you.

MAGGIE: (*Pause*) Thanks.

CHARLES: Stay for a round on me?

MAGGIE: I would, but I'm slammed, honestly. Goodbye.

LUCAS: Bye, Maggie.

CHARLES: Maggie—everything all right?

MAGGIE: Yeah. I'm fine. Really. (*She leaves the bar.*)

CHARLES: She okay?

LUCAS: Far as I know.

CHARLES: Well. Sorry I'm late.

(LUCAS, *still on edge, decides that he could use some air.*)

LUCAS: Not a problem. Y'know what—I'm starving. Are you hungry?

CHARLES: No.

LUCAS: I'm gonna go next door, get a sandwich. You want anything?

CHARLES: No, thanks.

LUCAS: You sure? It's better than Amtrak food. I'm starving. No? Okay. I'll be back. *(He exits.)*

*(*CHARLES *sits alone for a quiet moment.)*

*(*FRANK *enters and approaches the table with a drink. He puts the drink down in front of* CHARLES, *a practiced routine.)*

FRANK: Afternoon, Charlie.

CHARLES: Frank.

FRANK: How'sa boy?

CHARLES: I'm all right. *(Brightens)* Oh, you remember my friend, the one who drinks the gimlets?

FRANK: Yeah.

CHARLES: His cancer's in remission. Just found out this morning.

FRANK: Hell yeah. Bring him in, we'll get him nice and sauced.

CHARLES: Yes, we will.

FRANK: I'm likin the book this time.

CHARLES: Good.

FRANK: That last book was awful.

CHARLES: I'm glad you're enjoying this one.

FRANK: I know it's not our day, but do you want to…I could come sit?

CHARLES: Could we do it on Friday? I have to catch a train.

FRANK: Yeah. Yeah, of course, of course.

CHARLES: *(Reassuring)* Only because I don't want us to be rushed.

FRANK: Understood. Oh, hey! I can't believe I forgot— wait here! *(He exits in a hurry.)*

(CHARLES *drinks.*)

(*After a moment* FRANK *enters with a small model of a sailboat. He carries it with grace and great care. Eager for encouragement, he places the boat on the table in front of* CHARLES.)

FRANK: What do you think? I just put on the sails this weekend.

CHARLES: I'm very impressed. It looks good.

FRANK: Gotta start small.

CHARLES: Yes.

FRANK: Work your way up.

(CHARLES *notices something on the model, a detail.*)

CHARLES: Look here, though. You want to line up the back stay with the mast. And set the mainsheet here, so it can tack between port and starboard. Do you see?

FRANK: (*Encouraged*) Oh, yeah…

CHARLES: Just a small adjustment. You're well on your way, my friend.

FRANK: Thanks. I was hoping you'd like it.

CHARLES: I do. I like it very much.

(FRANK *watches with genuine concern as* CHARLES *drinks from his glass and then stares down into it.*)

FRANK: All right, sailor, you look like you need a joke.

CHARLES: I…I, I'm not sure.

FRANK: Have you heard the one about the pirate?

CHARLES: Ah…

FRANK: You'll like it: this pirate walks into a bar…

CHARLES: (*Giving in*) All right…

FRANK: This is good, no, listen: this pirate walks into a bar. He's got a peg leg, a hook for a hand, plus an eye patch. Bartender says, "What happened to your leg?" Pirate says, "Arrgh, it was a storm, I was knocked overboard and a *shark* bit me lower leg off!"

(CHARLES *is only half-listening to the joke, lost in his own thoughts.)*

FRANK: Bartender says, "Wow. What happened to your hand?" Pirate says, "A battle, one of the enemy cut me hand clean off". Bartender says, "Unbelievable. Well, what about the eye patch?" Pirate says, "A seagull dropping fell in me eye". The bartender's surprised, says, "You lost your eye to a seagull dropping?" The pirate says, "It was me first day with the hook".

CHARLES: *(Softly; to himself)* My God…

FRANK: I know. He said, it was his first day with the *hook. (Laughs)* That's rich. That is rich.

(Beat)

FRANK: So, the train, where you off to?

CHARLES: Maine.

FRANK: Huh. I could use a new parka, if you're anywhere near the LL Bean outlet.

CHARLES: Afraid I won't be. Supposed to meet one of the speakers from, ah, for my lecture series.

FRANK: Gotcha.

CHARLES: Between you and me…I'm not sure.

FRANK: About?

CHARLES: Going up there. Sitting down with him.

FRANK: *(Pause)* Well, it's like you always say. Go with your gut.

CHARLES: Right. Yes. Thank you, my friend.

FRANK: 'Course, pal. You let me know if you need anything.

(FRANK *exits, leaving the sailboat model on the table in front of* CHARLES.)

(CHARLES *is alone, holding his glass, staring at the boat.*)

(*After a moment—he takes a breath and blows softly into the small cloth sail.*)

(*The boat moves forward.*)

(*Lights down*)

END OF PLAY

www.ingramcontent.com/pod-product-compliance
Lightning Source LLC
Chambersburg PA
CBHW050757160726
48004CB00002B/599